The Gate in the Garden wall

Other Books by Sam Pickering

Essay Collections
A Continuing Education
The Right Distance
May Days
Still Life
Let It Ride
Trespassing
The Blue Caterpillar
Living to Prowl
Deprived of Unhappiness
A Little Fling
The Last Book
The Best of Pickering
Indian Summer
Autumn Spring
Journeys
Dreamtime
The Splendour Falls
All My Days Are Saturdays
Happy Vagrancy
One Grand, Sweet Song
Parade's End
The World Was My Garden, Too
Terrible Sanity

Travel
Walkabout Year
Waltzing the Magpies
Edinburgh Days
A Tramp's Wallet

Literary Studies
The Moral Tradition in English Fiction, 1785-1850
John Locke and Children's Books in Eighteenth-Century England
Moral Instruction and Fiction for Children, 1749-1820

Teaching
Letters to a Teacher

Memoir
A Comfortable Boy

The Gate in the Garden Wall

Sam Pickering

// Lake Dallas, Texas

Copyright © 2022 by Sam Pickering
All rights reserved
Printed in the United States of America

FIRST EDITION

Requests for permission to reprint material
from this work should be sent to:

Permissions
Madville Publishing
P.O. Box 358
Lake Dallas, TX 75065

Author Photograph: Edward Pickering
Cover Design: Jacqueline Davis
Cover image: "The Dreamer" at the Ruins of Oybin, by Caspar David Friedrich ca. 1835. Oil on canvas. Accessed via Wikimedia, https://commons.wikimedia.org/wiki/File:Caspar_David_Friedrich_011.jpg, 6/28/2021.

ISBN: 978-1-956440-10-2 Paperback,
ISBN: 978-1-956440-11-9 Ebook
Library of Congress Control Number: 2022937346

For Vicki or, as she is sometimes known,
Nurse Victoria

Table of Contents

ix	Introduction
1	Time on My Legs
23	A Tangle
37	8:00 in the Morning
49	The Old Oaken Bucket
82	Likeness
95	Radioactive
136	Everything
146	Solstice Sunshine
175	Notes
188	Endings
199	About the Author

Introduction

"In these days of almost universal insomnia any attempt to mitigate the sorrows of the sleepless cannot fail to deserve, if it does not obtain, the warmest possible welcome," Harry Graham stated in the preface to *The Bolster Book* (1910). "No apology therefore is necessary for the publication of a volume primarily designed to minister to the needs of all who are strangers to the arms of Morpheus. In the compilation of this Book for the Bedside, as I have ventured to call it, one single object has been resolutely kept in view. Every chapter has been chosen solely on its merits as an aid to slumber; every page, by reason of its irrelevance and discursiveness, is a natural soporific; every paragraph is calculated to induce sleep." Graham's goal is beyond my reach, indeed beyond the dream of every writer I know. No matter how resolute my intent and how verbs hobnail my thoughts, I sometimes slip. I lose my grip on meaninglessness and fall downhill, soiling sentences in the low ground of significance and shredding delight amid the stony till of high seriousness. It is difficult, however, to resist wondering about important matters, for example, snowflakes that burst into flame when they touch the ground then burn so intensely they heat the sky and melt future snows, turning them into rain.

    Of course what one person deems important strikes another as insignificant. For me ostensibly ignorable doings are more memorable than television and newspaper happenings. Amid the small, life flourishes. On Saturday Vicki and I drove to the McDonald's in Willimantic. There Vicki bought a birthday treat for the dogs, a McDouble to be shared by Suzie who is at least fifteen, Jack who is probably fourteen, and Mia who might be thirteen or sixteen. That night after removing the pickles and onions, Vicki stuck three small colored candles into the bun. She then handed me the burger, lit the candles, and photographed me while I held the treat and the dogs cavorted at my feet. "A Happy Birthday like those we celebrated when the children were little," Vicki said blowing out the candles and slicing the cake. "Our grand good life," I said. "Much has been taken, but 'much abides.' Let us hope that we don't become too withered and world weary to notice and appreciate."

Inconsistency is both the strength and weakness of the essay. Inconsistency reveals that a person is alive, shifting and moving, both breaking free from and embracing orthodoxy. Moods change like the seasons. One moment thoughts are overcast and rainy, the next sunny, the sky a blue porcelain bowl, white shadows nicking it here and there. In this book I look at things from different perspectives: inside and out, top and bottom. I find answers on one page. On the next page they become questions. Like the hero of the novel as T. H. Green described him, indeed like life itself, the essay is the sport of fortune, its weal or woe often depending on "the impression of outward things." Throughout these essays I enjoy myself although some things I describe are grim. Obliquely Harry Graham points the way, or at least I think he does. The cultural vertigo created by spinning platitudes about like tops delights him. The first stanza of "Virtue is Its Own Reward" asks, "Virtue its own reward? Alas! / And what a poor one as a rule! / Be Virtuous and Life will pass / Like one long term at Sunday-School. / (No prospect, truly, could one find / More unalluring to the mind.)"

Because essayists yearn to appear fresh and because "choral conversation" is boring, they celebrate originality. "We are free to think as we please, and so most of us cease to think at all, and follow the fashion of thought as servilely as we follow the fashion in hats," A. G. Gardiner wrote. Not unexpectedly Gardiner criticized education for forcing conformity. "We standardize our children. We aim at making them like ourselves instead of teaching them to be themselves—new incantations of the human spirit, new prophets and teachers, new adventurers in the wilderness of the world. We are more concerned about putting our thought into their heads than in drawing their thoughts out, and we succeed in making them rich in knowledge but poor in wisdom." How could responsible parents behave otherwise? People are herd animals. Occasionally, someone kicks the rails, tosses his reins, and races away in what at first appears a gallop but what time eventually reveals to be a slow trot. Chesterton once wrote that there were two types of people, "those who accept dogmas and know it, and those who accept dogmas and don't know it." Chesterton was wrong. All people accept dogmas and know it. Some people feign ignorance or pretend innocence while others refuse to acknowledge their conformity. Often the latter vociferously assert their independence, and in order to assuage their pride, stage displays for themselves or for others in hopes of creating fictional public, often political, personae.

Although Thoreau changed his wardrobe and

tailor when he camped beside Walden Pond, he was, Leslie Stephen wrote, incapable of altering the tenor of his thought and still lived "in the atmosphere of Cambridge debating rooms." "Far from being a true child of nature," Stephen stated, "he is a man of theories, a product of the social state against which he tried to revolt. He does not so much relish the wilderness as to go out into wilderness to rebuke his contemporaries." The devotion of Thoreau's disciples is often weedy and scratchy. But short of wandering the outdoors wearing jackets with uncountable numbers of pockets, combat boots, clothes not sewn by bespoke tailors, and bent under picks and shovels, test tubes, microscopes, hand lenses, a library of field guides, headlamps for the dark, bags for snakes, boxes for insects—all of which I have worn and carried—how does one become, not a child of nature, but escape the evanescent demandings of the self and become immersed in natural things seemingly beyond the ego? The person devoted to awakening appreciation and love for the natural world almost always reacts to or in concert with his contemporaries, be they books or people. In these essays I write signatures of pages about the outdoors. My Nature is, however, one of words, objects sketched into being by vowels and consonants. A local Leslie Stephen once admonished me saying my fondness for flowers and trees, birds, and the often overlooked crawling generations was admirable, but words were my real love. "For you affection begins with word at first sight."

In *Stray Feathers from Many Birds* Charles Dixon said, "the sermons preached by Nature in her lovely temple are full of beauty and simplicity; each of us is welcome there, the seats are free." Preaching comes easily to me. However, believing that congregants pay other than late-night, armchair attention requires a degree of hubris of which I am not yet capable. For my part, though, I cannot resist Ebenezer Elliot's secular homily, "To the Bramble Flower." "For dull the eye, the heart is dull," Elliot wrote, that cannot appreciate the beauty of the bramble's "tender blossoms." After the passage of years and brighter flowers ceased quickening remembrance, sight of the wild bramble, Elliot said, evoked "The fresh green days of life's fair spring / And boyhood's bloss'my hour." "Scorn'd bramble of the brake!" he exclaimed, "Once more / Thou bidd's me be a boy / To gad with thee the woodlands o'er, / In freedom and in joy." Today blackberries and raspberries grow year-round in groceries, in Price Chopper on the same counter as blueberries and strawberries. Once they were summertime rarities and grew in abandoned pastures or along the shoulders of less-traveled roads. They were country treats plucked by children and brought home in woven basswood baskets. They were not a "Product of Mexico" packaged in plastic containers each containing six ounces, special only when sold "Two for the Price of One." When I was afield gadding about, I always picked more berries than my family could eat. Mixed among them were worms and green stink bugs seasoning taste and conversation. Briars ripped my hands and arms, and after picking, my clothes were ratty and bloody. In fact the more blood the greater my glee and the bigger my appetite. What do cuts matter to a boy who has just seen two black snakes and almost stepped on a copperhead, when cicadas have serenaded him, and butterflies pirouetted about him like woodland sprites?

    Although Elliot's poem wasn't very good, it awakened sleeping memory. In this book I quote much poetry. Most of the verse is ordinary and like my life itself rarely rises to a lyrical peak. Some poems are instructive, others humorous but few inspirational. Canting uplift does not make me clap and shout "huzzah." Longfellow got things slightly wrong. Some, but not all, of life is real. Much less is earnest. I've never suffered from meddler's itch. Before humbug can dig under the skin like a chigger and cover itself with the scales of dead thought, I douse it with a mental anti-fungal thick with clotrimazole and scouring truth. To me, that stable of high school graduation speeches, Emerson's advice to "hitch your wagon to a star," seems akin to the similarly atmospheric but more gamesome "Hey, diddle, diddle" with its ambitious high-leaping cow. People bedeviled by vain imaginings of worldly success should avert their eyes from the heavens and hitch their wagons to lies. If they remain resolute and unscrupulous, the wagons may become Maserati's.

    I am bookish, and even on still days passing breezes blow leaves onto my pages. The leaves don't all slip from trees common in the woods of southern New England: oaks, birches, hickories, beech, and maples. Their origins are more diverse. Some are exotic; others waft in from different climate zones. Their conditions vary, too. A few are sooty with mildew having traveled long distances through time and place while others are green and fresh, their petioles never having broken from their nourishing stems. A fortnight ago a hundred-year-old advertisement for Holloway's Pills and Ointment appeared in my study. "The Pills strengthen the nerves, rid the system of all impurities and stimulate to natural activity the Liver, Bowels & Kidneys," the advertisement claimed. "They promptly cure Indigestion, Loss of Appetite,

Biliousness, Sick Headache, and kindred ailments. Females find them of the greatest value." If used "in combination with the Pills," the Ointment "will be found an unfailing remedy for all Skin Afflictions, Bad Legs, Old Wounds & Sores, Boils, Insect Bites, etc. It is also invaluable for Gout, Rheumatism and Sciatica; and gives welcome relief in most troubles of the Chest and Throat." Unfortunately, Holloway didn't claim his medicines could alleviate the distress of Reader's Gas or Writer's Cramp, Block, or Piles.

 In January I received an email sent from Tehran. "As you said in your book, letters to a teacher, I know you receive a hundred mail or emails per day," my correspondent began. "But I would like to say how much your reply would be important for me. I would like to translate one of your book to Persian and before contact with publisher I want to talk to you? how could it be possible? I'm waiting for your reply." For decades I've ached to visit Iran. I've longed to wander the dusty ruins of Persepolis and stand in the shadows beneath the great winged bulls with human heads that guard the gateway built in the time of Xerxes. I've imagined roaming Isfahan's Royal Plaza unseen and being happily alone in The Mosque of Shaykh Lutf Allah. A walking tour, Robert Louis Stevenson said, "should be gone upon alone." Ideally a person should be free "to stop and go on, and follow this way or that, as the freak" takes him. Of course, a person is never alone even if no other people are in sight. Dreams, hopes, fears, and memories accompany him, in my life great crowds. Sometimes they are silent, but often they chatter and shriek like rooks.

 My correspondent was not an internet fiction. He was real, and I replied that although I'd long admired Persian culture, he would have to work solely with the publisher, probably "an impossibility." I explained I was too old "to worry about the tangled problems of translation." I forwarded the notes to my son Edward who also admires Persian and Islamic culture. Each email soon seemed a tile from a mosaic. "Of course you shouldn't lift a finger to help with any translation," Edward wrote, "yet you could have been a bit more encouraging to your Iranian admirer." Edward said that Iran intrigued him, adding, however, "that much of my interest derives from Fitzgerald's version of 'The Rubaiyat' which may not be the least pertinent to modern Iran." "Probably not to the modern Iran of propaganda," I answered," but certainly pertinent to the Iran in our minds." "When twenty to twenty-five years from now, Francis, Eliza, and I are contacted by Iranian biographers, journalists, and hagiographers wanting to know more about the American essayist and college professor who, improbably, became the presiding spirit of Iranian pedagogy—a modernized and newly powerful Iran exerting itself on the world stage—I will think back to these emails," Edward wrote light-heartedly in his final Persian letter.

Writers hope that with the aid of divine reconsiderations their books will rise from the discard pile. Realistically, however, once dead, always dead. Books do not emerge from the dustbin with freshened spines and glowing pages, sporting wardrobes of zoot-suit jackets and two-toned black and white wingtip kickers. Generally, the only people who appreciate old books are the writers themselves. Life isn't a book, but books can make lives. When bored and at a loss for thought and idea, and indeed when I am sad, I often open one of the books I wrote thirty years ago. In flipping through its pages, I sometimes rediscover the past. Almost miraculously, the forgotten animates the present. Ten days ago, I read an essay describing flower beds I created when the children were little. Our yard is till and boulder, and for years I dug and crow-barred rocks out of the dell. To replace them I carted in wheelbarrows of topsoil from the woods behind the house. The flower beds are gone, pushed aside by other stones rising through the ground. Behind the house, however, is my rockpile. Its stones seem massive, few of which I could lift now. The pile will outlive my life and pages. Indeed, it is alive. Small creatures live in and around it. When I studied it as I did after reading about the flower beds, the present became the vibrant past, that time when perspiration flowed from me in rivulets and I glowed with satisfaction, that time when I handed small rocks to the children so they could "help" me, loading them into the little wagon I bought for them at a tag sale.

Occasionally, though, readers send authors unexpected gifts making writers hope that even though their books have gone to ground life flickers on a page or two. I collect presents not royalties. On New Year's Eve, Vicki and I received a tin of homemade cookies sent by Patricia, the wife of Dave Lull, an internet reader turned friend. Every December, Patricia bakes cookies for neighbors and family, this year forty-eight kinds of cookies. On the enclosed porch of their bungalow house, she erects three folding tables, each six feet long and two and a half wide. She places tins of cookies atop the table, so many stacks of tins that the tables shine like cities in a Flash Gordon film.

On the upstairs scale, the cookies Patricia sent us weighed 6.2 pounds. Eating them rapidly would have forced us into bariatric surgery. Afterward we'd have to visit the dentist so he could reduce our sweet teeth to the size of normal molars. Like an outline for an essay, Vicki developed a plan for eating. She arranged the cookies in platoons on baking trays. As they entered the maw of battle, the platoons crumbled and vanished. On my trays I mustered the chocolates while Vicki marshalled a division of treats: lemon squares, macaroons, sugar and peanut butter cookies, magic and coconut bars, poppy seed slices, and ginger snaps among many others. As we ate the cookies, the ghosts of Christmases and New Years Past came to mind—not thin wispy presences but full-bodied and rich on the palate and in recollection. Suddenly I saw the icing on Mother's coconut cake shining like silk, and I smelled the bourbon fragrance of Grandma's fruit cake. For her part, Vicki said that as she munched, she unconsciously lifted her hand to pour hard sauce over plum pudding.

In a recent book, I wrote that I hadn't tasted caviar in fifty years. An old friend who inherited enough money to dine well and derange her liver, sent me a tin of Beluga Sturgeon Caviar. Writing doesn't necessarily broaden one's views. Usually, it focuses and narrows. It makes a person opinionated and so curious he is petty. I am both ashamed and proud to admit I researched the price of the tin. To leap from water to land, from fin to hoof, metaphorically speaking, all I can say is "Holy Cow." The caviar wouldn't be at ease with the everyday munchies that hang out on my palate, so I have storied it in the pantry. Before an acquaintance drops in, I may set it on the kitchen table. Of course, I won't expose the tin at lunch time. Maybe sight of the caviar will add bounce to my pedestrian reputation, that is, if the person who notices it doesn't confuse the contents with tuna fish. In any case the container will be an artifact resembling a colorful phrase in dull sentence. Certainly, the caviar is too expensive an accompaniment for pizza and chicken tenders, and although I can't remember when I ate it, I don't recall admiring the flavor. Last year I read and enjoyed George Sala's richly-seasoned analysis of its taste.

"To acclimatize yourself to caviar," Sala advised, "you should begin on a course of Dutch herrings washed down by a couple of tumblers (taken fasting) of cod-liver oil. After that, empty a pot of black currant jam into a salt cellar, and cram the amalgamated contents into a sardine box half full of fish. Stir well and keep the box in a warm room for a fortnight. Then serve on butter and bread and tell me how you like it." Perhaps common-sensical gourmands should avoid ova and spawn as they could cause, as John Banester described in the seventeenth century "griping torments and gnawings or frettings of the belly." If culinarians devoted to goog experience "windinesse and blasting of the inward parts," they might do well to follow the old remedy suggested in *An Hospital for the Diseased* in 1595. "Take a quarte of Malmsie, and two spoonefuls of the pith of Parsley rootes, and a handful of Violet leaves, and five Bay leaves, seeth all these together into a pint, and drinke it morning and evening warme."

Nostalgia seeps through my essays as it does through the minds of all sentient oldsters. Their present moments are utilitarian; their calendars, red-lettered by doctors' appointments. The syllable gist appears so often in conversation that it deserves a group name like a glaring of cats or a cackle of hyenas. Older people spend mornings and afternoons with cardiologists, urologists, dermatologists, oncologists, ophthalmologists, and gastroenterologists. Gists reproduce rapidly, and as a person ages, he becomes host to an increasing number of Aesculapian gists. The salubrious gists that quickened his youth and middle age decrease, among them, tourist, humorist, and activist. Some gists are seasonal and disappear completely as a person ages, amorist being a prime example. Despite the medical gists that confine people my age to waiting rooms, sentiment still trickles into mood and thought. Not long ago on the radio I heard The Journeymen's rendition of "Lord, I'm five hundred miles away from home." I am sixty years and eleven hundred miles from my childhood home in Tennessee. In the song the singer laments not having a shirt on his back or a penny to his name. "Lord," he says, "I can't go back home this-a-way." I have dressers of shirts and banks of pennies, but I, too, can't go home. My this-a-way differs too much from the that-a-way I was. As I recalled the names of streets—Iroquois, Tyne, Chickering—I wondered why I left Nashville. Unaccountably, I remembered hunting rabbits on Aunt Lula's farm. I carried a twenty-gauge shotgun and wore an orange hunting jacket its breast pockets corrugated with shells. I pointed the gun but never pulled the trigger. One afternoon I stumbled on a still hidden in an old stone barn. Father wouldn't let me return to the farm for two weeks. When I went back, the barn was empty.

People are Jani looking first one way then before their lives have passed looking the other. As I now questioned my having left Nashville, I know I would have regretted remaining. If I had stayed, I'd have begrudged fantasies not lived. Maya Angelou's caged bird sings "of things unknown / but longed for still." In contrast, the free bird floats downstream and "dares to claim the sky." Many people ride the wind and dip their wings "in the orange sun's rays." Yet, as they age into weariness, their longing for stability and quiet predictability grows At this time some people romanticize the cages from which they fled. Only rarely, however, do they return to the playgrounds of childhood. The person who knows he can't go home again wishes that he could but is happy that he cannot.

Reaching a satisfying conclusion on a page is easy. One need only to herd words well. In life conclusions smack more of beginnings than ends. I have often said that I lie frequently. In October a young English teacher and aspiring writer wrote and asked why I didn't always "tell the truth." Because my questioner was naïve enough to believe that everything had a reason for being, I lied. "For pleasure and to make life interesting, appealing, and more meaningful," I answered, advising that if distortion made him ill at ease, he should write fiction. "It and occasionally nonfiction are socially and morally acceptable venues for fabrication." I also advised him to read. "Don't overrate the effects of reading, however," I cautioned. "Rarely does a book explain matters completely. At best it can make you reflect." Someday hence, I thought, my correspondent might run across Hazlitt's statement that "lying is a species of wit, and shows spirit and invention." What then will he think? In any case, the man wrote back by return mail. This time he asked me to recommend novels that "featured male vulnerability." Every male and female my age is vulnerable to sundry diseases. Among my friends the subject has been coffee-talked into a coma. When Parkinson's and Heart Disease are ringing the doorbell and a lawyer is advising a person to update his will, lachrymose psychological vulnerability doesn't matter.

"Don't reply. He's bulging with a litter of gooberish subjects," Vicki advised. "If you write, he'll respond immediately. Remember the epistolary tar baby in which you got stuck when you answered the letter from the Pentecostal who wanted to know what you thought about Jesus's being 'a mixed species,' his mother a Jewish woman born in Nazareth, 'his daddy, a God born and raised in Heaven.' Afterward every Holiness bishop in North Georgia prayed for your soul. Have you forgotten the Gorgon Bitch of the Universe? What was it she asked?" "I can't remember exactly, something about atheistic teachers causing head lice," I said. "I think it was ringworm," Vicki said. "Anyway, your answer provoked a handful of venomous letters. The careful person takes a sleeping pill before replying to a question from a stranger." Despite Vicki's warning, I answered the man's letter. I prescribed a sampler of swashbucklers, "literary multi-vitamins" crusty with imagination and spirit-building provender, mettle to buck up the enervated: Robert Louis Stevenson's *Kidnapped*, Walter Scott's *Rob Roy*, and C. S. Forester's Horatio Hornblower tales. When I was young, Father read me Forester's novels. Many nights I'd sailed into sleep as a midshipman serving under stout-hearted Horny and striding the quarter-deck of *Adventure*.

Of course Vicki was right. Two days after receiving my amphetamine-laced bon-bons, the man wrote back. "Do you know a remedy for existential depression?" he began. Next, he asked, "What is the most effective way to decolonize a classroom? I'm white, and should I stop teaching books written by people of color? Also, my department recently hired an expert in Queer Theory. I'm pretty sure I am heterosexual. Can you recommend a theoretical book for people like me?" I didn't answer the letter. "I'm no longer a schoolmarm. My literary dietician days ended a decade ago," I told Vicki. How could I explain what a long life has both taught and not taught me, lessons my correspondent may learn and understand only after decades of living? Moreover I've forgotten much that I once knew. After Father reached eighty, he lost his grip on the minutiae of life. In six months I will be eighty, and my hands are not as strong as they once were.

Three weeks ago, Benny, an eighty-six-year-old friend, fell in his kitchen and cut his head on the corner of a table. Benny lived alone, and it took him two hours to crawl to a phone and call the rescue squad. Repairing his head took eighteen stiches, and the next morning Vicki and I visited him in the hospital. Benny's wound was gory but superficial, and we had a good time, the highlight of which was a nurse's coming into the room and asking Benny, "What medicines do you take?" Benny is practically deaf, and the nurse had an undecipherable foreign accent. "I take *The New Yorker* and *The Nation*," Benny began, mistaking *medicines* for *magazines*. "I doubt the young man who keeps asking you questions would have enjoyed the visit as much as we did." Vicki said later as we walked across the hospital parking lot. "He's too ingenuous to appreciate the comedy of age."

For a while after I imagined hearing the whistle blowing five hundred miles away, I considered writing an essay entitled "My Guys" packed with colorful reminiscences. The problem, of course, is that the guys and the me I recalled have become other guys. Moreover, boys know boys, but men don't know men or women well. Life surrounds adults with protecting inhibitions and reduces the complex to the simple. It shapes lives suitable for obituaries but not for revelatory pages, at least not for those written by an aged guy raised on snips and snails and puppy-dogs' tails, but withal old-school and proper, at least mostly so. No boy escapes becoming a crooked man and at least once or twice walking a crooked mile. Unless they are anchorites all people live in crooked houses, but so long as they lean when they enter the front door and don't trip on the sill or bang their heads against the jam, they'll be okay. They will be even better if they follow the suggestions proffered by Betsy in a letter: "Be kind, treat people right, respect the planet and its occupants, do as little harm as possible." Betsy reads my books and is my age. She and her husband own a farm in Michigan. They have a dozen cows and eighty ewes. Betsy cards wool and last year knitted mittens for Vicki and me. I wear mine when I am outside except when I drive. I'm a nervous driver and always drive barehanded, my fingers gripping the wheel like pliers.

In one of his *Ruthless Rhymes for Heartless Homes*, Harry Graham wrote, "Late last night I slew my wife, / Stretched her on the parquet flooring; / I was loath to take her life, / But I had to stop her snoring." The poem does not reveal the cause of the woman's percussive sleep. Perhaps she drank too deep from *The Bolster Book*. Maybe she stayed up beyond midnight reading this book. I'm not sure, and I lack the energy to investigate the matter. A hundred and forty years ago in *Breakfast in Bed or Philosophy Between the Sheets*, George Sala judged, "From all that I can see, or hear, or am told, and from a little, perhaps, that I feel, I am inclined to apprehend that there is a good deal of Madness going about the world just now." In all ages "the majority of mankind are cracked." Maybe the most efficacious vaccine to protect one's self against this pervasive delirium and to keep white waistcoats with wrap-around arms out of his closet is to study the contents of these essays. Afterward pittering acquaintances may call a person a dunce, but that is just the dizzard's way of saying one is wise.

Intentions resemble kitchen doors. Eventually their hinges loosen, and when slammed shut, they tilt and allow air to whisper through rooms. Once a teacher, always a teacher. Or, to explain things in better words, as St. John said, there is a branch that "abideth in me." Occasionally it brings forth fruit, sweet albeit shriveled and cankered by time. A month after deciding not to answer my young correspondent's third letter, I recanted and wrote him. I said nothing about pedagogical matters. Today English departments inhabit an alternate universe, one from which literature has been purged and consigned to a distant realm of outer light. Politics matters more than poetry, and I avoid politics, heeding the sensible imperative, "Don't argue with blockheads. Stupidity is highly contagious." As a remedy for depression, I echoed Betsy's letter and urged the man to follow the advice St. Paul prescribed to the Philippians: "Whatsoever things are true, whatsoever things are honest, whatsoever things are just, whatsoever things are pure, whatsoever things are lovely, whatsoever things are of good report; if there be any virtue; and if there be any praise, think on these things." Did the young man write back? Yes, his reply was short. He didn't ask any more questions. He simply said, "Thank you."

Time on My Legs

A person worn out by the everyday might assume that errand-free, anti-social days concentrated energy and focused attention. But they do not. Instead, they scatter thought and generate purposeless movement. Every morning after putting the dogs out and eating breakfast, I retire to the study with a pot of tea and sit at my desk. I don't settle. I swallow a handful of mysterious pills then peruse the absence of email. Afterward I shift to an armchair near a window. I place the tea tray on the floor near my feet, lay a notebook and two pens on a table beside me, and begin reading. However, the day when I can sit with a book in my lap and read through hours has passed. After a chapter or, on disciplined mornings, two or three chapters, I'm on my feet. My dog Jack has adapted to my virus life by vomiting every morning between 8:15 and 8:30. At slightly after 8:00 I pick him up and carry him into the yard. If it is not too cold, I join him outside and stand on the stoop by the kitchen door until he recovers.

  I don't immediately return to the study. I usually brew a second pot of tea, recently Yorkshire or Lady London. I also get a snack, generally a clementine. The snacks vary, however, often influenced by what I see when I open the refrigerator door. Sometimes I munch a handful of olives, a stalk of celery, or a nub of cheese forgotten and moldy at the back of a shelf. Other times I'll notice a container of hummus and shovel out globs with Saltines or Stoned Wheat Thins. If Vicki has been forgetful and left a jar of peanut butter on the counter, I'll remove the lid and spoon across the surface careful to disguise my pilfering by not digging noticeable trenches. If a basket of snacks is atop the refrigerator containing Cheese Curls or Tortilla Chips, I'll investigate. I've perfected the domestic art of removing a handful of nibbles without decreasing the apparent size of the package. The truth is that I explore the kitchen endlessly. For me the kitchen is a close of small shops: bakery, confectioner's, cheese monger's, and green grocer's among shelves and cabinets of others. I peel grapefruit and mangos. I open coconuts and dig out the meat, adding color and tang with a relish of blueberries. I munch raisins, figs, apples, almonds, bananas, and if I can find them, Vicki's chocolate chip cookies. Yet, because I am not looking forward to anything, weeks fly by, all days seemingly the same. In contrast, when a person eagerly anticipates an event, time creeps and hours hobble.

    The back door beside the pantry ought to be a revolving door. I go in and out of the house every hour. I go on treasure hunts, or so I call them, looking for dog droppings. Thrice a day I pick up sticks and carry them to the woodpile in the back yard. In the afternoon I wait for the mailman even though I no longer subscribe to magazines or receive letters or bills. I bury compost. I trim hedges and trees that don't need to be trimmed, and I sit on a granite boulder in the back yard and rub Jack or worry about Suzie who has suddenly aged. She has lost her hearing and wanders aimlessly suffering from canine senility. Often, I cradle her in my arms. "An old man and his old dog," Vicki said last month. "Yep," I said, and rubbing Suzie's ears, silently serenaded her, singing my favorite dog song. It's an old-timer like me, "Granny, will yo' dog bite?" Suzie's pet verses are: "Chippie on the de railroad, / Chippie on de flo', / Granny, will yo' dog bite? / No, child, no! / Possum up a 'simmon tree, / Oh, my Joe! / Granny, will yo' dog bite? / No, child, no!" I wish I could recall fifteen years ago when Suzie was young and gay and imagined treeing opossums, but I cannot. Actually, maybe she was never frolicsome—no matter she has always been my dog.

I don't listen to radio, and only rarely do I turn on the television. Some evenings Vicki and I watch "Kingdom," a serial on Netflix, the main characters of which are Korean zombies. Unlike American zombies that can only stagger about and moan, Korean zombies have evolved. They scream louder than coloratura sopranos and because they can run faster than Olympic sprinters almost never fail to dine on prime cuts of human. Zombies, of course, cause less damage to individuals and to the world than do the Faustian creatures who dominate the news: among hearses of uninterred others, as my friend Josh describes them, "the Orange Man, the Scarf, the Colonic Masseuse, Three Necks, and then the Cardboard Men haunting state houses in South Carolina, Florida, Texas, Oklahoma, and North Dakota"—hucksters, jobbers, and place holders, the "decivilized," all sorts of blacklegs peddling barnacled thought and abscessed moralities, caitiffs who have thrived ever since fool-killers became endangered. "The people with whom a person associates shape character and determine reputation," Mother said. "Open your heart and wallet to the needy and the downtrodden. Be kind. Be decent. But bar trash from the door." In these latter days of isolation, one mustn't become so bored that he relaxes and allows corruption to creep into the mind through radio and television.

Although the virus has caused untold people to lose jobs, crooks continue to flourish, and their larcenous internet machinations occasionally break the tedium of confinement and entertain, causing the somnolent to blink. "Hey, you do not know me personally," Rouvin Zucker wrote. "But I know pretty much everything concerning you. Your personal fb contact list, smart phone contacts, plus all virtual activity on your computer for the past 172 days." "Rouvin must be an amazing guy," I thought. I wasn't sure what "fb" stood for, maybe "forgotten buddies." If Rouvin owned such a list, I wish he'd mail it to me. The past means a lot to oldsters like me. Many of my friends have disappeared. No matter how I search I cannot discover their whereabouts. I've sunk pipes deep into the ground and kneeling down have leaned over the open ends and yelled their names. But they never answer. If I had a list of their addresses, I'd sip a cup of kindness and write them for the sake of auld lang syne, especially now that the virus has provided me with so much free time. I've never owned a cell phone, but a fellow who knows about everything that I have written and that has appeared on my computer since November 17 is entitled to a slight mistake. For the mathematically addicted, Rouvin's note arrived on May 3, and I used the Gregorian, not the Julian, calendar to ascertain the date that he began to peek.

Rouvin said that my last perusal of "adult material pages" triggered his malware, and as a result he had a video of my indulging in self-love. "Remembrances of high-school romances past," Josh said. I wasn't sure what adult material pages awakened the censorious eye of Rouvin's malware. I have never looked at pornography, but admittedly, I occasionally read the *New York Times* online, and I knew that according to hordes of patriotic, gun-worshipping voters that's a perversion worse than the behavior of the Good Samaritan. No matter what activated the malware, Rouvin was so shocked and repulsed that he demanded I atone for my imposthumed antics. In America, money washes away sins and paves the way out of Purgatory. Unless I mailed him $3000 worth of bitcoins in the next two days, Rouvin said he would "nail me to the tree" and send copies of the video to three people on the list of my correspondents. Among them might be my "boss, co-workers," and parents. Retirement stripped me of bosses and co-workers, and my parents died thirty years ago. But, oh, how I ache to see them. If Rouvin can contact them, then he is an angel, impure and fallen, but nevertheless one of the winged tribe. Alas, Rouvin probably cannot work miracles. He concluded his email by asking that after he mailed the video to my correspondents, "Will you be capable to gaze into anyone's eyes again? I doubt it." "Silly fellow," Josh said shaking his head after reading the salutation. "He is terribly naïve. That video will be the social making of you. Not only will you be invited to make countless lucrative appearances, but you will be importuned to run for high political office."

    Internet acquaintances from pre-virus times write me. They still wear the same black hats, rather black foundation garments. They assume that because of being isolated I am at loose ends and accordingly more susceptible to spam than in the past. "Olga from Kiev" sent the identical note she mailed eight years ago, the only difference being she lived in Moscow then. "Hi," she began. "Remember me? How are you?

Still no message from you! I miss you actually! When will we go out for a date? I'll be waiting for your suggestions and I hope that our meeting will happen as soon as possible! Please answer me!" The virus has not made me lax, but it may have affected association, causing a low-grade peculiarity. After I read Olga's email, Oliver Herford's short poem "The Milk Jug" inexplicably came to mind. Perhaps I thought about the poem because instead of being tawdry, it's humorously wholesome and domestic. Moreover, unlike kittenish Olga, the poem's narrator is an actual kitten. "The Gentle Milk Jug blue and white," the kitten begins, "I love with all my soul / She pours herself with all her might / To fill my breakfast bowl. / All day she sits upon the shelf, / She does not jump or climb— / She only waits to pour herself / When 'tis my supper-time."

"I wonder what poem you would have remembered," Vicki mused, "had your correspondent identified herself as Eulalee." A verse drizzling with sentiment, I said, something like John Trotwood Moore's "O Momma, I'm a-coming, / Save that lullaby for me / For I'm a-longing, just a-longing / For a grave in Tennessee." "People who ignore social-distancing will probably realize that wish," Vicki said. "Not if they are vaccinated," I said. "But a vaccine doesn't exist," Vicki replied. "Maybe one does," I said, quoting a Holiness prescription for biofeedback, "Jesus is the vaccine."

As a person ages the synapses in his brain short-circuit, and the mind, if it is a kingdom as Edward Dyer wrote, becomes a strange or, better perhaps, whimsical dominion not always ruled by will and reason but often under the suzerainty of the inexplicable. Neither Vicki nor I has ever smoked, and during the forty-five years, we've lived in Storrs, no one has smoked in our house or yard. Yet, twice during the past six weeks the smell of cigarette smoke awakened me at three in the morning. The aroma was strong, and on each occasion, I got out of bed and searched for the source of the smell. I went through every room, upstairs and downstairs, and into the attic and basement. Thinking that a stranger might be prowling the yard looking through widows, I grabbed one of Edward's old baseball bats, went outside, and walked around the house. I did not see or hear anyone, and when I eventually returned to bed, I woke Vicki. "Where is that smell coming from?" I asked. "Who do you suppose is smoking cigarettes?" "What smoke? What cigarettes?" Vicki said. "I don't smell anything. Be quiet and go back to sleep."

Quiet hours force a person to confront his inconsistencies. The shameless contrivances of the televised revolt me. When the elderly read Shakespeare, they read the comedies and avoid the tragedies, consigning them to the young and inexperienced. Not only do the old recognize aspects of themselves in King Lear, but in his broken wanderings, his misunderstandings and faulty judgments, his lonely and guilty plight, they see fragments of their lives, both the lived and the imagined. For my part, I could not bear to read *King Lear* again; yet when I listen to the evening news, I hear Edmund's angry rant, "This is the excellent foppery of the world, that, / when we are sick in fortune,—often the surfeit / of our behavior,— we make guilty of our / disasters the sun, the moon, and the stars: as / if we were villains by necessity; fools by / heavenly compulsion; knaves, thieves, and / treachers by spherical predominance."

The elderly are fractious, and although political

pettifoggers nauseate me, I don't react well to the benevolent assurances of the kindly. Verbal hugs repel me. "Epiglottal spasms of promiscuous affection," Josh calls them. "Sham pharmacopoeia. We are not 'all in this together,'" he remarked quoting a treacly editorial in the local paper. "Social distancing legislates seclusion. I have never been a professional communitarian, and I refuse to be initiated into the order of the clean limbed and living," he added. "In fact, many of the nicest people I know are a little musty. But under no circumstances, viral or bacterial, will I muck about with the unbrained." Writing immunizes a person against both the baneful and what Agnes Repplier called "untempered sanctimony." Arranging living into paragraphs separates one from events and causes everyday anti-social distancing. Whether one's paragraphs are melodious or cacophonous doesn't matter. Writing isolates, and if Josh wrote more, his reactions to sophisters and the foolishly opinionated would not be as strident and he'd probably sleep sounder. A fortnight ago he telephoned me at midnight. He'd heard a television sawbones blame a sudden increase in the number of suicides on social distancing. "Rubbish," Josh said. "Suicides flourish when guns are cheap and easily obtainable. Repealing gun control laws increases suicides much as spreading manure on a corn field in the spring enlarges the yield." For Josh, television never lies fallow. No matter the season, it's ripe with food for indigestion. Last month he reported that he'd watched an interview with a local woman whom the virus liberated from an overbearing domestic overseer. Toward the end of the interview, the woman became teary, looked dolefully into the camera, and said, "I know he is looking down on us now." "I went to school with the man," Josh said. "He was a bastard, and if he is looking in any direction, he's looking up."

Age also isolates. Byron got things slightly wrong in his lament "So we'll go no more a roving." Time clogs the heart with plaque. People become forgetful and are not "still as loving." Hearing fails, and the distant no longer sings alluringly. Vision clouds. The moon is not "still as bright," and if one goes roving, he will probably become lost. For me the restrictions imposed by the epidemic are a continuation of those caused by aging. The difference is that the virus has intensified awareness of isolation. Moreover, it disrupts habitual patterns of thought and while narrowing behavior diffuses purpose. Recently I unaccountably interrupted a rice cake safari to the kitchen to tell Vicki about Mohammed's affection for his favorite cat Muezza. According to story, Muezza was sleeping on the sleeve of Mohammed's robe when Mohammed heard the call to prayer. Rather than disturb the cat, Mohammed sliced the sleeve off. Afterward he slipped on the rest of the robe and went to pray. "A nice story," Vicki said, "but I wouldn't cut the hem off a good dress for Suzie. But who knows? Cat people are different from dog lovers."

Nowadays, I don't elaborate thoughts. I didn't respond to David's inquisitorial "what" after I speculated that societies in which country clubs were important institutions were not only more civilized than those dominated by churches, but they were also more moral. I ignored an email from Josh in which he suggested that universities change the mealy phrase student-athlete to the more exact entertainer-athlete. On my not immediately answering the email, Josh fleshed out the concept, even though he knew I avoided meat. Coaches, he said, should be considered impresarios while the entourage of assistants, life-skills managers, and haberdashers were the equivalents of conductors, ushers, and stagehands. "Of course, entertainers must be paid, the amount dependent upon their majors and their progress within the majors." Such recompense had to be "fair and sensibly utilitarian." After graduation some degrees, Josh observed, "are considerably more valuable than others." Consequently, during their performance years, the salaries of entertainers whose studies could be monetized immediately after the termination of their studies should be less than those paid to teammates whose studies "led to the dole." Among majors generating lucrative incomes were, for example, combustion engineering and neurobiology. Among those occasioning markedly less remuneration were sociology, political science, family studies, psychology, and English.

Although intrigued by an old schoolmate's writing me, saying that youth should be viewed as a period of postpartum dementia, "generally, but not always, going into remission when a person reaches thirty," I didn't rise to the behavioral hook. I sighed when a childhood friend wrote observing that in rereading *The Great Gatsby* he noticed that Gatsby frequently repeated the phrase "Old Sport." "Who did I know in the remote past who would say to me from time to time 'Old Sport'—none other than Sammy The Boy!" When things that go around come back around, they are always different. Old, we are, I thought as I read the letter, "but neither of us was ever a real sport. We were too studious and responsible." As for Sammy, decades ago he mutated into a good man in the worst sense of the word, as a florilegium of social commentators have put it, describing the inevitability of time's transforming the lively and the free-thinking into the conventional and predictable, people comfortable with apathy and easeful convenience—too upright for the good of others. And The Boy? He was but one of the crowd of people I'd been, and the nostalgia I felt for him was sensibly short-lived. I jotted down my friend's address so I could send him a lulling copy of my most recent book. "Acetaminophen for isolation fever," I wrote on the title page. That afternoon I cycled to the post office and mailed the book. Afterward I tossed Old Sport's letter into the recycle basket.

Only occasionally did a passing remark provoke more than two sentences. From Bulwer-Lytton's *Pelham*, I copied an observation from a drawing room conversation, "Poetry is for the multitude, erudition, for the few. In proportion as you mix them, erudition will gain in readers, and poetry lose." "Yes," I agreed. "Modern lyrics explode like cherry bombs. They dazzle but vanish like the evening flash of lightning bugs. The poems people enjoy are old-fashioned recitable narratives. Plodding through tale and morality, they offer continuance, and community, poems about characters like "naughty Brier-Rose" and "Leadville Jim." No listener ever resisted falling in love with "sure-hearted Jennie McNeal," black-eyed Jennie McNeal true as steel. "No drunkard lies under the daisy-strewn sod!" I began, reciting the final stanza of "I Have Drank My Last Glass," "Not a drop more of poison my lips shall e'er pass, / For I've drank my last glass, boys, / I have drank my last glass." One example of poetic good behavior leads to another, and I remembered the bridge keeper who closed an open drawbridge and prevented the "lightning express" from plunging headlong into a river. He chose to fasten the bridge before trying to rescue Willie, his "golden-haired darling." As the train approached, Willie fell into a whirlpool and was drowning. Do your duty, the keeper's tearful wife whispered, urging him to tend to the bridge first and preserve the passengers, "And Heaven will help you / to save our own darling from Death!' "There, sir! That's my story, a true one," the keeper recounted, his cup overflowing with thanks to Heaven for enabling him to pull Willie out of the water. "Though it's far more exciting than some, / It has taught me a lesson, and that is, / 'Do your duty, whatever may come!'" I mulled writing an essay about oilcloth and "Home Sweet Home" poems, but I didn't. I went outside and picked up sticks, on the way stopping in the kitchen to fortify myself with a handful of "reduced fat" Triscuits.

 The virus has not made me completely careless and undisciplined. Later in the day I sent a card to a man soon to celebrate his 88th birthday. I wrote two cards. Depicted on the first was a straw basket overflowing with pink and white tulips. The illustration was mellow and muted, appropriate for an old timer's birthday. The inscription inside the card wished the recipient "a beautiful day and a year full of happiness," a sentiment I echoed in the note I wrote. I thought I was done, but I wasn't. After addressing the envelope, I turned the card over. It had been printed for the Alzheimer's Association, not the right card to send an ancient of days, I thought, as I crumpled it into crow's feet and frown lines. Vicki's leukocytes are more assertive than mine. At the first sign of lumpy sentiment, they rush to restore salubrious reason. "You should have mailed the first card," she said. "Your friend is half blind. Even if he noticed

Alzheimer's, he wouldn't have known the meaning of the word. Did you forget that he is eighty-eight and doddery?" Vicki is bolder than I am and throughout the epidemic has only partly curtailed her shopping. Twice I've cautioned her about bringing the virus home from the grocery along with the shredded wheat and grape-nuts. "If I catch it and die," I warned, "I won't forgive you."

My unfocused life has been a swirl of unrelated things. One morning a forgotten schoolmate sent me an anecdote he copied out of a two-hundred-year-old schoolbook. "'Mother,' said little Mary Ann, 'why do you cry so much?' 'Indeed, my dear,' replied her mother, 'I have great cause to weep since your father is dead.' 'But mother,' said the child, 'you need not weep so much. God is still good to you.'" That afternoon I read Melville's *Typee* while simultaneously listening to *La Boehme*. The opera and the book resuscitated dead associations and brought a miscellany of things to mind. From the singing of the bohemians arose memories of people I knew in younger days, "The Passing Parson" and "The Professor of Everything." Neither was a roustabout. Both were bright and hardworking, respectable and admirable—lively people I knew when sobriquets were complimentary. Most of the roving I did was fanciful and like the present beyond imaginative possibility. As I read *Typee*, I recalled a boyhood dream of wandering Polynesia, not in the company of Tom's "gentle nymph" Fayaway but with the prosaically named Martha. Although homespun, she was so beyond my aspirations that she might as well have inhabited "some fairy region."

Did I once own a talking bird who wore a crown of daisies and had invisible orange tail feathers? Did it fly away after I abandoned cloud land for school?

Probably, I mused, its being unable to endure classrooms raucous with Mac's didactic yapping and Muff's moral mewing and spitting. "No," Josh said, "it was the Auk of the Covenant and left when you stopped winning prizes in Sunday School." Did golden lizards ever bask in the sun atop my head? If memory serves, they did, but then memory does not serve as well as it once did. It has aged into an unruly servant. Like an ancient retainer it has grown too familiar with its master to pay close attention even when summoned by a ringing bell box. I'd like to imagine that in my ear lobes I wore plugs made from mother of pearl and that tattooed down my back was a magical tree. Because it changed with the seasons, budding and blossoming in spring, becoming a wall of leaves in the summer, a scarlet and orange afghan in fall, and a trellis hung with snow in the winter, the tree was clearly a native of North America, not Polynesia, probably a maple. No trace of the tree, not even a remnant of taproot, remains. Perhaps it didn't flourish in my imagination, but for someone my age, the actual is relatively unimportant. Besides, unlike the truths of fancy, literal truths incapacitate and render people unfit for many things: teaching, marriage, fatherhood, and certainly isolation.

Immediately before the lockdown, I read Katherine Boo's *behind the beautiful forevers* and Richard Flanagan's *The Narrow Road to the Deep North*, the latter winner of the Man Booker Prize, the former the National Book Award. The sad music of humanity reverberated through the books—the deep chords of complicated kindnesses and the melodies of guilt and calloused self-preserving neglect and maltreatment. I read the books on sunny days before possibilities diminished. Isolation changed my reading. Medea told old people that boiling could restore youth. Of course, it didn't. Although Ancient Abigail lost flesh and bone, she did not become laurel-eyed Gayle skipping to the tune of zip-a-dee-doo-dah. For my part I read down. I did not return to childhood, but I read books written for children and adolescents. They lightened isolation and did not pluck at my emotions. I never placed one a bedtable and closing its covers slowly murmured, "no, no."

People are their own greatest mysteries. All the books I read during the epidemic were shelved in the study, but how most got there puzzled me. A few probably came from library fund-raisers and or closeout sales. For all I knew, others crept into the house during summers when Vicki and I were in Canada, their pages momentarily clumping together into shankless legs. Several belonged to Vicki's father. When he was small, relatives gave him collections of Indian stories and animal fables. Later he received swashbucklers: accounts of pirates and derring-do on the high seas, of frontiersmen in buckskin, knights in chainmail, of mysterious islands, and of explorers lost in sandstorms or feverish in jungles. In *Typee* along with a label from McClelland & Co., a bookstore in Columbus, Ohio, was a small gift card reading "Merry Christmas, Edward from Dr. Powell." Vicki's father was born in 1911, and he probably received *Typee* three of four years after his grandmother gave him a copy of *Kidnapped* in 1919. Like me. he probably read *Kidnapped* and its companion tale *David Balfour* when he was ten or eleven.

Typical among the books which enabled me to navigate the doldrums of isolation was Cornelia Meigs's *The Trade Wind*. Published in 1927, *Trade Wind* was the eighteenth volume in Little, Brown's "The

Beacon Hill Bookshelf," a gathering of books "which because of their approved quality and appealing format would prove an ideal library for boys and girls." The story took place under storm clouds gathering on the eve of the Revolutionary War. Thirsty for excitement and life, young David Dennison sailed with Andrew Bardwell out of Benton Harbor in a schooner. They sneaked away from Massachusetts avoiding a British frigate and afterward roamed the Indies and the western Mediterranean, trading and seeking funds to purchase a shipment of guns to prevent their being sold to British troops in North America. As devotees of sea-faring novels written for adolescents could expect, they were successful, not without enduring rough, but sanitized, seas, not the kind of surf that surged through Boo's and Flanagan's books creating emotional undertows. After hardening years at sea, David returned to Benton Harbor. As he sailed through reefs and shoals on a breezy spring morning, David "looked up at the rocky headland, at the smooth green of the new April grass that crept up to the gray of the rocks; lifted his eyes to the white rolling clouds in the blue sky, where the gulls were circling like dull flecks of silver, and said in his heart that this spot, of all the places in the world, was surely the very fairest." Waiting for him was his childhood sweetheart, fair Janet, a sunny-eyed schoolteacher. This being a boys' book, David did not marry Janet—alas. The wind of war blew him back into the Atlantic as master of the Patriot, a privateer. Accompanying him were the memory of Janet and the actual presence of Adam Applegate, an aged buccaneer and bye-blow descendant of both Billy Bones and the Ancient Mariner. In boys' books sailing toward the Happy Isles is soporific. Waves may swell, but the dark broad sea doesn't gloom. Moonlight is golden, and the sounding furrows are silent, just the literary bromide to lull the fretful and the isolated to sleep. As reading down is a nostrum lessening the hippish feelings of virus days, so looking down is a herbal restorative dispelling the gloom of isolation. Down in the soiling dirt is where most gods live, rooting and flowering, dying, and being reborn. Dogma flourishes in arid heights. The gods who live upstairs beyond the clouds are abstractions, absences transformed into doctrinaire, often inhumane, presences by deluded, self-serving followers. The fragrance of Korean spice viburnum cures mawkishness more effectively than any nostrum found in a sanctified book, quicker even than Hungary Water's rosemary and wine. On Saturday Vicki and I walked our Vale of Enna along the Fenton River. We didn't see Persephone. But she was nearby. The perfume of autumn olive swirled around her like incense. Fans of redbelt fungus whisked zephyrs gowned in many colors about her: glistening oranges, reds, grays, and daisy-whites. Wood thrushes and rose-breasted grosbeaks sang for her; phoebes bounced up and down to glimpse her, and her footprints bloomed with flowers: demure anemones, trout lilies and wake robins nodding in obeisance, and then coltsfoot and bellwort. To prevent their disclosing Persephone's presence, the clappers, Vicki said, had been removed from the blossoms of the latter and boots muffled the hooves of the former. A ruffle of flowers bordered Persephone's path: pussytoes, twin leaf, its petals prim and starched like the dress of a nurse, appropriate for a plant often known as rheumatism root, gay wings, and marsh marigolds in vernal pools formed when the goddess leaned down and rocked backwards on her heels to examine something: a painted turtle sunning by the river on a mat of winter sweepings or a snapper just crawled out of a marsh, a spatula of damp black mud glistening atop her shell.

"There's scarcely a street in old London," Leigh Hunt wrote 190 years ago, "perhaps not one, from some point or other of which a tree may not be discerned...keeping his tranquility, like some old thinking philosopher or innocent child, in the thick of the smoke and noise." From the blinding smog and the utilitarian tallies of calculators—the dead, the sick, the recovered—trees are a respite, natural cordials: in the forest a small beech arrayed for a bridal in last year's leaves white and fragile as lace, nearby new buds on other beeches, lance-like, two or two and half inches long, and almond and caramel. Once they begin to swell, their bud scales peel up and back into wings. In the presence of the scarlet twigs of Japanese maple, the exalted status of numbers vanishes. Seeing is different from counting. Seeing immerses while counting separates by creating abstractions and in the viral world of the hospitalized and dying is ineffectual and desperate. Deep woods are shipwrecks of broken spars and masts. Although the trees are dead, they are paradoxically alive, quick with mosses, ferns, and mushrooms, bone polypore, hoof fungus, and layered chicken of the woods, among others. They are home to zoos of creatures, beetles, shrews, chipmunks, snakes, and opossums. No sculpture can capture the beauty of broken trunks, cankered and eroded into totems of cavities, cracked by drought and frost, and leaning lop-sided, heavy with nappy burls, their barks stained by rusts and shredded into gray, blue, black, yellow, and orange. The magnificence and beauty of wreckage stop feet and mind: the sight of a huge white pine match-sticked across a trail or the limbs of an oak shed like clothes inconvenient on a hot day

After a certain age, many things appear paradoxical. People attend funerals, not to mourn the deceased but to discover who among their mutual acquaintances are still alive. A person realizes that what initially appears inconsequential is actually meaningful. The obituary of John, a long-time philosophy teacher, did not lose the man in a briar patch of achievements or an almanac describing years past. Instead it was short, ending with the loving, revelatory statement, "John kept bees for 40 years and had a number of other quirks, all of them harmless." Small knowledge gives great pleasure while great knowledge gives small pleasure. I had my teeth cleaned two weeks before the virus began to spread. During the scraping I asked the hygienist how many mouths she'd seen in her career. "Hundreds and hundreds," she said, before pausing and adding that many patients greeted her on the street and in stores. "I never recognize them. Their faces are always unfamiliar, but if they'd open their mouths wide, I'd know them right away." She also told me that in twenty years of cleaning teeth she had only been bitten once.

Yes, the last shall be first. Walks are also paradoxical. They are balms, not despite but because of the presence of Death. Unlike the numerical skeletons on the news, in the woods deaths intrigue and enliven. Last week beneath a birch reduced to a sleeve I found the desiccated corpse of a downy woodpecker. The bird had been dead since fall, and because the remains were neither damp nor odiferous, it must have recently tumbled from a socket pocking a limb. I put the bird on a shelf in the garage next to a jar containing the tail of an opossum I also found in the woods. Yesterday I found the entrails of a large rabbit. A red-tail hawk or maybe a fisher unzipped the rabbit, ignoring the offal and leaving the intestines wrinkled and folded like links of sausage. The only other bits I found were tufts of hair and the animal's powder puff tail. I also stored the tail in the garage.

  I don't keep all the remains I find. On Sunday in a cave formed when layers of a granite bluff buckled, I found the skull of a deer. Two sets of molars remained in the jaw, and the skull was dry and papery. I climbed the bluff and showed the skull to Vicki before placing it in my back pack. "No," she said, taking the skull from me. "I'm returning it to the cave. It belongs there, and putting it back will please the forest spirits." On returning from the cave, she quoted Barry Cornwall's poem "A Chamber Scene": "Tread softly—softly, like the foot / Of Winter shod with fleecy snow / Who cometh white and cold and mute, / Lest he should wake the spring below." "Unseasonable, but good cautionary advice, especially in woods haunted by old gods, goat-footed Pan and Cybele with her drum," Vicki said. "A little out of date," I said. However, I soon changed my mind. Napping in the side yard when Vicki and I got home was an almond colored buck. He had a massive neck, thick as a culvert, and his antlers were full and golden in the setting sun. On hearing us, he turned his head but did not leap to his hooves. Later he drank from the bird bath after which he glanced at the house then regally walked away. "Back to his forest," Vicki said.

  That night Vicki called my scraps in the garage, "Elementary school voodoo—ingredients for a magic potion to repel the virus." Vicki was closer to the truth than she knew. For me numbering is pedestrian, not magical, thinking. Moreover, much to my regret, the words I use and the places I inhabit are defanged—sterilized and devoid of hexes and curses. Would that when I saw a snake curled atop a flat rock, I believed the sight a harbinger of good or evil, although to be truthful snakes always make my spirits bound. If I saw a snake every morning while eating breakfast, I told Vicki, the bunions caused by isolation would fall faster than soufflés. "A strange metaphor," she said. "What do you expect?" I answered. "The homebound behave in peculiar ways. They rarely talk to others. Instead they talk to themselves, and trite, expected phraseology vanishes from their speech."

Today after dinner I read Thornton Burgess's Mother West Wind's "How Stories." "I am particularly interested in "How Old Mr. Toad Learned to Sing," I told Vicki beforehand. What also intrigued me was how the book got on my bookshelf. Written on the title page in pencil in big wobbly preschool letters was "Tommy G Rayo," a mystery boy. After I stopped reading, we watched another episode of "Kingdom." The screeching was cacophonous. But that was not unappealing. Often the only sound that a woodsy person hears amid the silence of isolation is that of an imaginary chainsaw guillotining in the name of progress. Atop the coffee table I put a couple of slices of apple pie and a few hunks of cheddar cheese, a biting intellectual varietal. Then when my attention drifted, I wasn't forced to mount a snack hunting expedition and rummage the kitchen. I had considered setting out a half dozen Milano cookies and a platter of purple grapes. But wandering the woods awakened a poetic culinary mood. "Of all the delicacies which Britons try / To please the palate or delight the eye," William King wrote at the end of the seventeenth century. "Of all the sev'ral kinds of sumptuous fare, / There is none that can with Apple pie compare."

A Tangle

At the beginning of *Jorrocks's Jaunts and Jollities*, Surtees banished Indolence, calling her "a slug-begotten hag" who drained the marrow out of imagination and fattened "on the cream of idea" before it floated "on the milk of reflection." Georges Simenon wrote at least five hundred novels. He also stated that he slept with ten thousand women. Busy people sleep less than the indolent, but they exaggerate. Simenon's second wife said the number of females was closer to twelve hundred. Barbara Cartland wrote 723 novels and when the going was good dictated eight thousand words a day. In comparison to her, I am indolent. I've only written 32 books, four and a half percent of Cartland's total. However, Surtees got things wrong. Indolence preserves marriage. During the forty-one years Vicki and I've been married, aside from Suzie's youthful frolicsome days when she occasionally jumped into my bed begging to be rubbed, the number of "friends" who shared my pallet was .083 percent of Simenon's corrected total.

Conclusions deduced from statistics are usually false. Vicki and I aren't layabouts. This spring we spent two days cleaning trash out of Mirror Lake. The lake is the eye of the campus and suffered from macular degeneration. While the slopes surrounding the water were green and light, the lake itself was a fetid brown absence. In past years it was home to a miscellany of creatures and creaturely thoughts inspired by snakes, birds, insects, and greenhouses of weeds and wildflowers. Across the shallows of the lake grew a cattail forest clogging spillways but also filtering runoff and sheltering nest builders like muskrats and boisterous red winged blackbirds. Sometime earlier in the year "green" thinkers poisoned the cattails. The shallows turned into mudflats heaped with whitened dried stems and refuse dumped by people unable to imagine the lake sacral. Instead of the budding and nesting life that awakened appreciation, people saw a wastewater pool, its gutter unskimmed and cluttered with the shells of turtles and sunfish lapping belly-up.

In the best of beautiful times humans pollute more than they create. At the end of spring semesters past Vicki and I removed trash from the shoreline of the lake. We donned Wellingtons and worked afternoons after class. In part I hoped students would recognize me as a faculty member. Maybe, I told Vicki, our example will teach more about good living than the lessons on my assignment sheet. Hope is naïve, but it stretches muscles and mind, and Vicki and I enjoyed the work. Educational musings aside, we scoured the shoreline on behalf of others, observant or not, and then perhaps more importantly for ourselves. Male widow skimmers patrolled the vegetation. Sometimes they paused in midflight and treading the air studied us making us feel a part of something greater than any page, indeed greater than ourselves. Eventually university groundskeepers took over, and not until this spring did we clean the shoreline again. Probably because the virus caused graduation to be suspended, and visitors ceased appearing on campus, groundskeepers neglected the shoreline. Accordingly, Vicki and I extracted our boots from the basement. Armed with a tool Vicki made fifteen years ago, a twelve-foot-long pole with a scoop at one end and a rake at the other, we marched off determined to remove all the rubbish we could reach. We cleared sixty pounds of garbage: bottles, books, rugs, bags, beer cans, balls, and sheets of water-logged plastic The work exhausted us. Leaning, pulling, and lifting, hovering over banks, trudging through gunk, isn't easy after a person has reached tottering age. When we finished, the shoreline was clean. For our part we were tattoos of cuts and blood. Our clothes looked like dirt daubers' nests. Our muscles throbbed and jumped spasmodically, and our skins burned and stank. Yet, we had shed inaction and felt refreshed and, to be truthful, a little self-satisfied. "Why," Vicki asked as we trudged home, "have we never seen other members of the faculty and the administration picking up trash? Certainly, whatever they spend their hours doing is less important."

Indolence has much appeal. One morning last week I got up at 4:15. I dreamed that I was in a group of several hundred people waiting to board a huge airplane. Passengers in the waiting-area were instructed to remove their shoes and leave them off until boarding began. On putting them back on, I discovered that another passenger had mistakenly taken one of my shoes and left one of his. To find my shoe, I was forced to crawl down the aisles of the plane and study everyone's feet looking for a mismatched pair. One-third the way down the left-side aisle, somewhere in business class I said, "To Hell with my shoe. This is too damn hard. Anyway, the welt was becoming unstitched." I then woke myself, got out of bed, went downstairs, brewed a pot of Yorkshire tea, and began reading *The Lost World* by Arthur Conan Doyle. Because of coronavirus, town and university libraries are closed, and readers must make-do with ordering books online or, as in my case, with volumes lurking dusty and unread about the house. Vicki's father gave *The Lost World* to Vicki's brother Alex on his tenth birthday in 1959. The book described a fictional world hidden deep in Amazonia. It was the sort of world boys at the end of childhood dream about and the maps of which they lose as they grow older. Almost inevitably, schooling cuts down luxuriant rain forests and in their place, plants crops of conventional careers.

For an indolent adult, the book was relaxed reading. It didn't preach or cause thought to ferment. How nice for an octogenarian to escape the pressing awareness that his skein of years is fast unraveling. How pleasant to read a book that encourages wandering, not through a land that Time forgot but through a land that makes one forgot Time itself. In the dozy hours before the sun rises on another fretful day, how refreshing to explore a make-believe world accompanied by Edward Malone, a lovesick newspaper man. Despite being "expected to get his first rugby cap for Ireland," Malone was moony and his spirit was mizzling away. Although he didn't immediately realize it, Malone ached for adventure, a pain the leaders of an expedition to the Amazon quickly ameliorated. The leaders themselves were the sorts of men met only in imagination. The titular head of the expedition was the famous zoologist, Professor George Challenger, an irascible "stunted Hercules" endowed with an "overpowering" presence and intelligence. The professor's head was enormous. Even so it seemed too small to contain his ego. While his face and beard resembled those of an Assyrian bull, his chest was bigger than a barrel, and his shoulders spread like a yoke linking a team of oxen. Instead of talking quietly, he bellowed and roared. His righthand man and boon companion was Lord John Roxton. Besides being extraordinarily wealthy, Lord John was a devotee of fine art and cigars, a renown explorer, a big game hunter, and "one of the great all-around sportsmen and athletes of his day." Avoiding the careless tread of iguanodons, fending off flocks of pterodactyls, battling prehistoric ape men, and escaping ambushes laid by brutes whose faces resembled those of giant toads with "warty, leprous skin," and loose mouths "all beslobbered with fresh blood" enabled readers to forget their pillbox lives and palliated nagging concerns about biopsies, leaky gutters, and broken lawn mower blades.

Crooks rise with the sun, and much of my daily reading focused on a morally lost world. After consultations with, among others, the Secretary General of the United Nations, and the "African Union Organization," James Emmett, the Chief Executive Office of HSBC bank in London wrote to discover if I was still alive. A Mrs. Cindy May, an American Citizen, Mr. Emmett reported, "came to our office with an application stating you gave her the power of attorney to be the beneficiary of your outstanding funds. She made us to believe that you are dead and that she is your next of kin." Before releasing any of the $21 and half million dollars swelling my account to Mrs. May, Mr. Emmett wanted to ascertain the state of my corporeal presence or absence, and whether I ever gave Mrs. May the power of attorney to represent me. Mr. Emmett was admirably conscientious and wrote me twice. Alas, age has made me slipshod, and I neglected to send Mr. Emmett my legal name, current address, cell phone, and Social Security number as he requested. Anyway, I am too old to be initiated into the lodge of the "Noovo Rishe," as George Ade put it.

Today privacy is rare, and the lives of most people are open rolodexes. My health interested several correspondents. Unlike Mr. Emmett who wanted to know if I were a goner, a decent man in Willimantic sent a hand-written letter inquiring about my spiritual health and assuring me that if I were a true believer I'd never vanish completely. "Do you think the dead can ever live again?" he asked and enclosed a "tract that gives comfort for those who are grieving and explains God's promise of bringing the dead back to life." From another stranger I received a broadside describing the "Powerful Kundalini Yoga mantra for healing. "Ra Ma Da Sa Sa Say So Hung," the broadside explained, taps "into the energies of the sun, moon, earth, and the Infinite Spirit" and "is an attunement of the self to the Universe that invokes a deep healing effect."

I have never been a ticket-buying fan, but now I am the holder of season tickets to doctors' offices, not something that makes me leap gleefully. I'm not alone. Almost all my older friends are beside me in the stands shaking medicine bottles, waving insurance cards, and practicing death rattles. Last month my old high school friend John telephoned. He is eighty-two and suffers from a ward of debilitating ailments. "I am so tired," he said. "I want to find my mother and ask her to make it all better." Not all my medical moments are dark. Amid the moribund lurk salutary comic episodes. Recently Dennis a former student of mine received an advertisement from Neptune Cremation Services. In the packet was a card stating "100% Service Guarantee" and promising to refund the client's money if he was not satisfied with "our services." The services did not satisfy Charlotte "Char" Cole, Dennis reported, and she wrote a letter "holding the company's feet to the fire" and demanding a refund and a full restitution of her body, this last so she could take her business to a more responsible crematorium and, of course, have hands with which to receive the refund. Instead of an afternoon cremation as she requested, her cremation started at 11:00 when she was suffering from breakfast dyspepsia. Moreover, she stated, "I found my quarters to be cramped and rather stuffy, the new pine smell far too over-powering to be pleasant. Small touches such as a bright fabric on the inside of the coffin would make all the difference, especially if scented with fragrancies of the deceased's choosing—may apple, fresh linen, old saddle, or passion fruit."

Charlotte's letter was detailed and certain to garner the refund that she requested. Among other matters she'd instructed that she be cremated "feet first in order to feel the wave of warmth sweep over me as my ashes rise to heaven, but I was placed in the oven head first. Facing backwards in any moving compartment, such as a train or car makes me ill, and the nausea from moving down the conveyor belt to the oven nearly made me lose my breakfast, especially with the bout of dyspepsia still roiling my stomach. Not the farewell I had hoped for!" Included among her complaints was one specific to her experience but which is generic to all crematoria. "Upon my incineration," she wrote, "my ashes were commingled with those of a loathsome cat someone had cremated before me and those of a disagreeable gentleman who was the loan officer at a local bank. I'm a very private person and do not like my ashes being mixed so lasciviously with others during this final intimate experience." Particularly galling was that the music played during the immolation was not Charlotte's choice "He the Pearly Gates Will Open." Instead the person manning the Hibachi played a rap song by someone named Watt. "Get high, get lost in paradise / This feeling's all we got tonight. / Baby, I'm a burning man, baby. / Burning man, baby."

Shortly after reading Dennis's fanciful letter, I received a package from a graduate school friend. He was retired, but for years he taught in the English department of a college in Virginia. In the package were offprints of articles he wrote about "Eastern" nature writers, people whose works I admired, not just Thoreau but lesser-known figures like Charles Conrad Abbott and William Hamilton Gibson. Along with a short account of his own life and health and descriptions of the fortunes of his children and grandchildren, my friend included a "statement of purpose" composed by the new vice-president of his college. "Regrettably probiotic—heavy boilerplate that sinks thought," my friend wrote. "Dr. Johnson said that after ideas go, style remains. What is left after both ideas and style go?" The vice-president's statement was constructed not written, and slogging through it was the impacting wordy equivalent of traipsing through the sludge surrounding Mirror Lake. "My goals," the man wrote, "align with those of President Barnstable in supporting life-transformative education, enhancing research, and driving economic growth in the state. I am eager to approach these goals in ways that are relevant to all disciplines within our academic community: prioritize diversity, equity, and inclusion for our faculty, staff, and students, and approach our path forward with a strong interdisciplinary, innovative, and entrepreneurial spirit. I have had the privilege of many great conversations over the past few months and what I have learned is central to how I am approaching the role of vice-president. After extensive discussion, evaluation, and consultation with the exceptionally talented and dedicated team in the Vice-President's Office, we have decided to undertake a reorganization to maximize service to our faculty, staff, and students."

The corruption of man, Emerson wrote, is followed by the corruption of language. The vice-president wasn't corrupt. He was well-meaning. Today, however, the corporatization of language leads to the corporatization of people and their institutions. Language that purports to say everything but really says nothing despoils. "As we degenerate," Emerson wrote, "the contrast between us and our house is more evident. We are as much strangers in nature as we are aliens from God. We do not understand the notes of birds. The fox and the deer run away from us." When paragraphs of dry verbs and nouns are too much with me, I look out the window. I don't discover God or see abstractions, but I become aware of my surroundings, and melancholy and loneliness vanish. "Nature," Emerson said, "is made to conspire with spirit to emancipate us." Or as Charles Dixon, the ornithologist put it, "The pleasures derived from woods and fields are no fleeting ones; they leave a long train of golden memories behind them, and furnish stores of intellectual food which may be drawn upon perhaps when Fate has removed the observer from the country scenes he knew and loved."

Recently on the campus I noticed English Hawthorn in bloom, the Crimson Cloud cultivar, the white centers of its flowers shining like stars sunken in scarlet skies. I also noticed red vein enkianthus, its carillons of creamy yellow bells streaked with pink, dangling and chiming silently, delighting the uncramped mind. Not all that was lovely thrived. Near the enkianthus a massive copper beech was dying like many oldsters from the top down. The trunk of the beech was seventeen paces in circumference and had served generations of students as a lover's diary into which they carved their initials and those of their sweethearts. Across a path verticillium wilt was killing an adolescent tulip tree. Between their veins, leaves turned red and yellow then curled and fell to the ground, leaving branches wispy and forlorn.

In "The Flitting," John Clare wrote, "I love the verse that mild and bland / Breathes of green fields and open sky, / I love the muse that in her hand / Bears wreaths of native poesy, / Who walks nor skips the pasture brook / In scorn—but by the drinking horse / Leans o'er its little bridge to look / How far the sallows lean across." Clare's declaration of affection for the mild and seemingly ordinary, for green fields, forget-me-nots of wildflowers, and for pausing while crossing a small bridge and gazing about rather than hurrying onward is an apologia for what the worldly wise might think indolence but is instead a prescription for peace and harmony, healing thought, and a good life. Recently I've spent afternoons in full intellectual idle sitting in a folding chair in the driveway. I sipped tea and nibbled slices of Vicki's apricot bread. Jack stretched out on his side under the chair, and Suzie crouched beside me on all-fours looking like a small black sphinx. To my right a familiar assortment of birds splashed in the birdbath: robins, catbirds, cardinals, and phoebes bobbing their tails. Earlier in the summer cardinals nested in the yew by the back door. I watched them carefully worried that a feral cat might discover the nest. No cats appeared, and then one morning the birds disappeared—mother and father and the fledglings—gone without a goodbye. Perhaps, the cardinals on the birdbath were my birds, and when they fluttered in the water, they were waving to me. My presence wasn't disturbing. Like Clare's willows I didn't move so much as simply be. Carolina wrens jingled. Chipmunks scampered across a stone wall, and squirrels glanced at me then went about digging nuts from the ground. A small pickerel frog clung to a log, the yellow lines penciled down each side of its back brighter than an oboe. One afternoon a red-tailed hawk landed in the red maple by the drive. It perched on a low limb twenty feet away from me for half an hour. Occasionally, the bird rotated its head and glanced at me, but mostly it dozed.

    Late in the afternoon the sun shone low through the mugwort by sidewalk transforming the plants' inconspicuous leaves into glowing natural sculptures resembling decorations carved into the arches of Gothic cathedrals. In the broken light minute insects suddenly became visible. While some spritzed and darted in a white fizz, others blew and floated like they were riding droplets of helium. Occasionally, I raised the barrel-shaped lid of an imaginary Saratoga trunk. I moved slowly studying the hinges and hasps on the trunk. Sometimes they were tin, other times brass. Always Greek gods appeared on them in relief, usually Demeter or Dionysius, but once on a trunk that had belonged to a veteran of the Boer War, Ares wearing a pith helmet. As befitted the trunk's age, it contained thoughts that I once considering sewing into essays but which I neglected so long they became fusty and moth-eaten. Looking at a scrap of paper, I wondered who said, "The truly virtuous never make declarations of virtue." In what forgotten novel did the main character say to Miss Cynthia, "woman are queer creatures"? "Yes," Miss Cynthia replied, "they are daughters of men." In what essay, I wondered, did Artemus Ward write about a teacher in Salt Lake City who absconded with all the students at a ladies' boarding school? Beneath a sketch of an ancient tale, I wrote "the scientific mind." In the story after being told ravens lived two hundred years, a noodle bought a raven at the bird market in order to test the validity of the assertion. Books ago when religion interested me, I should have quoted Agnes Repplier's observation that many "devout Christian communities" expended "their time, money and energy extinguishing in the breasts of other Christians the faith which has sufficed and supported them."

On another scrap of paper, I'd written the last verse of George Linnaeus Banks's "What I Live For." "I live for those who love me, / For those who love me true, / For the heaven that smiles above me, / And awaits my spirit too; / For the cause that lacks assistance, / For the wrong that needs resistance, / For the future in the distance, / And the good that I can do." The poem once was very popular. After the verse I scrawled a hasty comment, "Oh, dear." I didn't write the endnote because I thought the verse poor, but because I envied Banks's decent clarity. I admired his visible heartfelt intention. I wanted to have done with the complicating academic inclination to discover shadows in cloudless skies. Among other papers I found a paragraph pondering what the dogs thought about Vicki and me. The speculation didn't go far. "Those whom dogs love," I wrote, "die old." Suzie and Jack have been with us for a third of our married lives, and at times treat us as if we were their offspring. Whenever we raise our voices in anger, they rush into the room and stand between us, changing our mood and making us feel ashamed.

I didn't rummage through all the loose sheaves in the trunk. Many of the excerpts and notes I wrote no longer interested me; however, in great part I stopped because native poesy distracted me. The yard was white with wreathes of clover, and the limbs of Carolina silverbell hung over the end of the driveway like a shawl two-plied, soft, and cozy. Not all the verses were bright with blooming, but their lines clung to eye and memory. Time and runoff from the salts slathered on Hillside Circle in winter killed the flowers I planted, scores of Iris and hundreds of daffodils. Day lilies vanished from a big bed near the road, and the only plant that has ever grown there are a few weak tendrils of poison ivy. I never dig them up because by summer's end they wither and die. Only one of my peonies remained, and it struggled to produce a single bloom. Amid pachysandra on a slight slope far from the runoff, Jack-in-the-pulpits spread slowly, almost as if monitored by an ecologically concerned chapter of planned parenthood. The Jacks had left their pulpits and the seeds produced by their flowering had not yet swollen and turned red, but above each plant a sheltering umbrella of three broad leaves spread wide.

Most of the flowers planted in the yard were not native. Still, like Clare's verse, they made moments poetic. By the back door stood two shepherd's hooks. Hanging from one was a pot of gay black-eyed Susan vine; from the other, lofus scarlet with horns: cornets, trumpets, and trombones. As I rested in my chair, the sound of worry dissipated. Mia bounded out of the house and jumped into my lap. As I stroked her back, I listened to the plants Vicki bought at Ledgecrest and potted beside the hooks. They were so ordinary that busy people could not hear them. But for someone indolent like me they were musical: double-blossomed yellow marigolds, fat purple coneflowers, a cuphea or firecracker plant, and two calibrachoa or million bells, one with red blooms, the other with red and yellow blooms looking like pastilles of hard candy. How nice it would be to believe, as Emerson wrote, that "the invariable mark of wisdom is to see the miraculous in the common." But, of course, Emerson overstated. Life is a tangle of letters and stories, moods, frenzied activity, indolence, hopes and worries, thready pink hardhack, the retiring flowers of spotted wintergreen, and, above all words, eventually followed by silent, contented passing.

8:00 in the Morning

By eight in the morning my day is done. By then I've indulged in walking rest for three hours. Rest is not something men my age get much of in bed. An assortment of ailments wakes them throughout the night: cramps bolting from foot to thigh, interminable trips to the lavatory, and the sharp mincing pains of peripheral neuropathy. Night sweats turn some men into faucets, their stopcocks opening and shutting. Perspiration soaks their pillows, and they shed their blankets. Afterward they become chilled, scoop up the blankets, and burrow under them cocooning themselves. I wonder if one of the old standby patent medicines could bring sweet sleep and mitigate the unpleasant nuisances of aging, say, Widow Welch's Female Pills, celebrated for winning a Certificate of Merit at the Tasmanian Exhibition held in 1891. Better, however, might be a Magneto Corset. "My Magneto Corsets," Mr. Ambrose Wilson testified a hundred and twenty years ago, "are Nature's Remedy for Rheumatism, Gout, Sciatica, Lumbago, Nervous Troubles, Mind Wandering, Loss of Will Power, Involuntary Blushing, & scores of similar ailments." "From the moment when you put them on a ceaseless stream of Magnetic Power permeates your whole body from head to heel. The joy of New Life, of New Health, and New Vigor thrills through every nerve." Mr. Wilson didn't mention night sweats, but surely, they'd be classed as one of the similar ailments.

Moreover, tottery age causes sundry other aches, and maybe a corset would add magnetic power to people's strides and stabilize their balance.

Two weeks ago I lost my footing and tumbled off a stepping stone crossing a stream. The stream was dry, and I could have easily strolled across the bed. "Why didn't you?" Vicki said in exasperation as I lay curled on the ground. "Are you in love with pain?" I fell on my left side banging a shoulder and a knee and wrapping my ribs around a loaf-shaped rock. The throbbing was unwelcome but familiar. Three and a half years ago, I wrecked my knee hurrying downstairs in our old farmhouse in Nova Scotia. Two years before that a stone wall on which I was standing collapsed, pitching me down a slope. My right thigh hit the ground first landing atop a rock which rose from the dirt to greet me. For six weeks my thigh was black and orange, looking like chocolate pudding into which someone had stirred curdled cream. A dozen years earlier, I slipped on an icy cut under Horsebarn Hill and doing a half somersault plunged into a creek bed caroming off two rib-breaking boulders. After this latest fall, the pain in my ribs radiated through days and was acute when I went to bed, hammering my chest whenever I turned or bent. Vicki doesn't like her sleep disturbed and instructed me to have the ribs x-rayed. "I've had too damn many x-rays recently," I replied. When I stand straight and walk, the ribs don't hurt, transforming roaming the house into ambulatory sleep. Moreover, after a good tramp, I don't feel discomfort when I sit at my desk.

I am not alone. The before dawn shift of house rovers outnumbers that of mall walkers. Rovers are generally aged and have retired not only from jobs but from ambition and what Aldous Huxley labelled "organized distraction." Vast organizations, Huxley wrote in the early 1920s, provided people with packaged distractions "which demanded no personal participation and no intellectual effort." "Fast-food intellectuality, heavy on the salt and awash with ketchup," my friend Josh said this year and cited packaged spectator sports and television imbecilic with its sensational menu of murder, carnival acts, pop music, and underdone situation comedies, all turning the brain obese and lethargic. Democracy might go the way of the Romans, Huxley speculated: "the Romans who came at last to lose, precisely as we are doing now, the capacity to distract ourselves; the Romans who, like us, lived on ready-made entertainments in which they had no participation. Their deadly ennui demanded even more gladiators, more tightrope walking elephants, more rare and far-fetched animals to be slaughtered." Huxley testified that the "political situation" filled him with "chronic horror." He said that he felt "the sensations of Gulliver in the paws of the Queen of Brobdingnag's monkey—the sensations of some small and helpless being at the mercy of something monstruous and irresponsible and idiotic."

If Boswell had not been a great fool, he would not have been a great writer, Macauley wrote. Only after a person has lived long and been force-fed endless helpings of balderdash seasoned with commonplaces, can he understand Macauley's statement. Being foolish protects a person from deadening convention and enables originality. How often does one hear and see people genuflecting to the smarmy phrase "make a difference?" The phrase is a feel good placebo. The one thing it doesn't do is make a difference. It oozes treacle, transforms thought into devitalizing feeling, and undercuts rational salubrious reform. Does a day pass without reading the phrase "our thoughts and prayers are with you," a statement that costs nothing and isn't worth anything? As people become early morning walkers, oddities which they eschewed fifty years ago in order to become successful attract them. Corporate managers no longer hover near spreading mayonnaise over their lives. No longer do they think and act mechanically. They cease noticing celebrity and front-page puppets. They'd rather discuss the doings of the "Old Man on a Hill, / Who seldom, if ever, stood still; / He ran up and down, / In his Grandmother's gown, / Which adorned that Old Man on a Hill." If the Old Man's alpinist days ever end, then perhaps the economy boosting habits of the profligate from Kilkenny who spent all his money "in onions and honey" might be appealing. In any case I know they'd enjoy listening to the Pelican Chorus. Afterward, they are bound to feel spry and be eager to kick a soccer ball around with the Pobble who has no toes.

A person cannot ignore the present snake-oil landscape in which companies tout cure-alls for ailments ranging from constipation to toenail fungus. "You will enjoy this," Josh said. Suffering from colitis caused by overdosing on television, he read medical textbooks, from one of which he sent me George Derby's "Antidote for Fleas." "One hundred percent effective," Josh wrote. "Boil a quart of tar until it becomes quite thin," Derby instructed. "remove the clothing, and, before it becomes perfectly cool with a broad flat brush apply a thin, smooth coating to the entire surface of the body and limbs. While the tar remains soft the flea becomes entangled in its tenacious folds, and is rendered perfectly harmless."

Moreover the tar will soon form a hard, smooth coating impervious to the insect's bite. If one is bitten before the tar is prepared, there were simpler ways of dealing with attacks of "these little pests." "On feeling the bite of flea, thrust the part bitten immediately into boiling water," Derby instructed. "The heat of the water destroys the insect and instantly removes the pain of the bite."

Before he retired, Hiram, one of Josh's fraternity brothers, was a hedge fund manager. Now he lurks behind a homey privet hedge. Hiram does not construct portfolios but invents. His latest project is sartorial, designing and marketing coronavirus masks to be worn by corpses who attend open-casket funerals. The masks do not promise to forestall the unlikely, that is, corpses spreading the disease by breathing on mourners, and the reverse, mourners breathing on corpses and infecting them. What the masks do is alter appearance. All the dead must do to pass incognito through their days is strip off their masks. The visible nose and lower face turn a cadaver into an unrecognizable stranger. Attired in a mask makes dear dead Daddy immediately identifiable.

Hiram advertises his masks in funeral homes, employing mannequins laid off from department stores as models. At a financial sacrifice, he refuses to paste billboards in the naves of churches as undertakers do for a small fee in South Carolina. "I don't think money-changers should paper the temple," he told Josh although the broadsides were advertising light, saying benign things like, "Jesus and the Folks Here at Braxton Memorial Love You. We are Your Family," "Give Your Beloved a Sanctified Good-Bye. Go Clemson," and "When You Are Tired of It All and Ready to Move to the Promised Land, We Are Here to Help Your Loved Ones Tote." For fly bait who were stylish dressers before Death swatted them, Hiram has a line of conservative masks in herringbone, tweed, and seersucker patterns. For sports addicts, he creates masks displaying the numbers on their favorite athletes' uniforms. On another mask appears the address of the deceased. "Reassuring relatives," Hiram explained, "that if their beloved goes walkabout between the chapel and the grave, he'll be found before the embalming fluid leaks out." The fee for individualizing a mask is small, and the possibilities, Hiram said, are almost unlimited. However, he wrote Josh, "I refuse to degrade my artistic talents and produce pornographic masks." Since the majority of corpses were lemmings in dress and behavior, Hiram receives few requests for personalized masks. What astonishes him is the large number of relatives who wish to identify their kin as Democrats or Republicans. Among the former, particularly among the liberal, St. Veronica and the Sacred Heart of Jesus is surprisingly popular. Ardent Republicans favor the depiction of an old-fashioned squall, raining, not cats and dogs but pattycakes of leprous brown matter. Among the customized masks, Josh's favorite is one crafted for a shoe hoarder, a woman who died owning six hundred pairs of shoes. On the mask shoe boxes are piled atop one another, creating model skyscrapers and the outline of a city, each box resembling a different floor. On the ends of the boxes appear an interminable list of shoe companies, to name but a few: Alexander Wang, Ipanema, Free People, Gucci, and Zodiac.

For people my age making up the past is easier than remembering it. Moreover, it's a good remedy for chronic fatigue. As every social weatherman knows, intellectual slopes are slippery, and once a person begins to ponder, predicting the result is impossible, that is, aside from sleep. Certainly, however, the truths of one day or generation are not those of the next, and fanciful accounts are often more real than the actual. The predilections of old stagers for the non-existent and for individuals whom society labels bad company are greater than those of youth whose reveries are framed by the materials of the everyday, the posts and beams of work and family worry. What morning walker does not imagine striding into a life impossible to have led? "There is a great deal lost in being born out of date," Agnes Repplier wrote. Cecil Rhodes "must have realized that the reign of Elizabeth was the reign for him," she added. "What freak of fortune thrust Galileo into the world three centuries too soon, and held back Richard Burton's restless soul until he was three centuries too late?"

"What makes trips out of time and place difficult," Josh wrote, "is that people can live nowhere other than the present. No matter how repulsive they think the phrase carpe diem, escaping the moment is impossible." Josh isn't quite right. Some mornings I travel to other places and to other times. I'm not an explorer, a scientist, or swashbuckler, and my travels are confined to a yesterday more immediate than three centuries in the past and to a tomorrow much closer than three centuries in the future. December has arrived. This year Vicki and I won't celebrate Christmas. Although the virus has made travel risky, the real reason we'll skip the seasonal festivities is that we have exhausted the energy of our middle years. Physically and mentally, we are unable to clean, decorate, furnish the groaning board, and paste carefree expressions on our faces. On the other hand Time does not always move linearly. Days revolve and parts of the past reappear and dislocate. Taped to a window of Dog Lane Café last week was a notice announcing a meeting of SDS, Students for a Democratic Society, an organization dated and as forgotten as round molds of tomato aspic. "Build the Student Movement Against War, Racism, Sexism, Xenophobia, Homophobia, Transphobia, and Tuition," the notice urged. "Tuition?" Vicki said. "Yes, alas," I said. "Give me that old-time radicalism. It was good enough for me. Sisters in the Eastern Star are more revolutionary than these student activists."

Age imposes conformity of thought and deed. Vicki and I are not alone in withdrawing from Christmas. "The coronavirus has kept people at doorknob's length," Tom wrote. "Fall has been restful. For the first time since I became a widower, my hours have belonged to me. When acquaintances invited me to their homes or said that they planned to visit, I replied, regrettably of course, that I'd love to see them but that I'd been exposed to the virus and was being quarantined. I haven't had a social drink in months. I haven't gagged suppressing a reply to a cretinous remark. I haven't dipped a shrimp into a clotted bloody sauce or washed down a tray of dreadful nouveau hors d'oeuvres, all the while praising my hostess for her adventuresome taste. Miracle of miracles, I've caught up on my reading and my bedside table is clear—at least until the next trip to the library." Tom added that he was going to "reuse the quarantine card" to avoid Christmas. "I'll say that I am one those unfortunates who despite rigorously adhering to the suggested guidelines has been exposed to the virus yet again. Just my bad luck."

Tom's note aside, Vicki's and my succumbing

to the demands of our diminished selves has made me lachrymose, and as I walk through the house, I recall the past—Christmases I spent with Mother and Father seventy years ago in Nashville in the Sulgrave Apartments. The Sulgrave has been razed, but on my travels, the swinging door from the kitchen still opens into the dining room. In a corner of the room stands my Christmas tree, and Winkie my cat is wearing a new red collar. As I sample Mother's pear and alligator pie salad, Father hands her a cup of eggnog. While standing in the imagined room, I remembered the first stanza of Elizabeth Akers Allen's once popular "Rock Me To Sleep, Mother": "Backward, turn backward, O time, in your flight, / Make me a child again, just for tonight! / Mother, come back from the endless shore, / Take me to your heart, as of yore." Fifty years ago I read the poem as background for a course focusing on the Victorian age. Then Allen's sentimentality made me queasy. Time changes taste, and diet. What was once undigestible soothes. Now the poem's simplicity appeals to the nostalgia of morning walkers aching to recollect the familial past.

Oh, the years are many, and the years are long, as Eugene Field wrote in "Little Boy Blue." But on my travels four decades haven't passed since Vicki and I first celebrated Christmases with the children in Storrs. Whiffle the little toy dog is actually in the attic, but on my walks, he isn't covered with dust. A little paint may have flecked off General the toy soldier, but he isn't red with rust. Downstairs in the living room, Francis is Captain Fatness. Edward is making small picture books describing the life of George our dog, and Eliza is reading through a library of books written by Edgar Rice Burroughs and dreaming of meeting Tarzan.

Sometimes I travel to the future. Edward's wife Erica is pregnant, and I imagine Christmases in which I sit in an armchair and cradle a grandchild. I see the smile of a little face and feel the touch of a little hand. That probably won't happen. I have exceeded my allotted three score and ten years, and the First Cause rarely doles out bonuses of extra years of good health. Alas, I suspect that despite being packed into boxes, our decorations already know that this December they won't escape the attic and adorn our house and moods. I envision them in the dark yearning to hear the angels sing "that glorious song of old." Missing their annual excursion to the little town of Bethlehem will make their hearts ache. I picture them wailing in disappointment and know they are wondering what has become of the people who "put them there." Oh, how they will miss the tree, the mantlepiece covered with snow, and the table tops on which they frolicked. When I imagine how they, and we, will miss us all, laughing and smiling, just sitting, our faces radiant with love, I become weepy.

It is now 9:00. Vicki is out of bed and stirring about in the kitchen, and my walking rest has ended for the day. The threadbare proverb "nothing is certain to happen except the unexpected" would be more accurate if it read "except the unexpected and the expected." The morning is sunny. Last week in the wood behind the dog fence, a vixen dug out an old burrow that has been unoccupied for three years, its entrance plugged by leaves and sticks. I put a bowl of kibble on the lip of the burrow, and I must amble along the fence and see if the snack appealed to the fox. At the moment outside the study, bluebirds are flicking through a hickory's low branches, and blue jays will soon be gabbling and bounding back and forth from limbs to the ground. Chickadees glean the lilacs, and Carolina wrens carol and cock their eyebrows at me. Watching birds increases happiness, an old saw states, not because birds teach but because they divert. As a result people who study them have less time to meddle and resent. Inactivity generates contentment better than activity, Josh sometimes argues. What a person does not think about and doesn't do makes him happier than what he actually mulls and does. "Mindless is contentment more."

Still, I wonder how I'd react if during some copperhead evening in the spring, I saw a Semandah. Climate change has altered the avian landscape. Accidentals have become common. The Semandah is a native of the Malabar Coast. But perhaps a wild Elephanta Wind will burst the pressure systems binding it to India, and like a tramp hopping a freight, a Semandah will ride a cyclone to Connecticut. Mating pairs are sacrificial, and their nests are fireplaces. Semandahs stack their nest high with wood. Afterward they strike their bills together like flints until they produce sparks. Eventually the wood catches fire resulting in an immolating flame which burns the birds alive. The pair study the weather and time the blaze so that a soaking rain douses the fire before it completely consumes the nest. What remains is a pudding of ashes. After a two-week incubation, brown worms, usually two but at the most four, bore out of the ashes. Once in the sunlight, the worms generate wings. They cling to the residue of the nest until they are fully fledged. Ornithologists are not sure what the nestlings eat during this period. In the intellectual life there is always a smidgen of entertaining mystery. The most widely accepted belief is that the ashes absorb some of the marrow and mucilaginous parts of their parents' bodies and that these in the form of small cindery tidbits nourish the young birds.

Later this morning I will walk along the Fenton River. Wings of foam feathers will curl in the eddies and flutter light and breezy. Virgin's bower has gone to seed. The filaments wrapping achenes are gray and loose and look like the hair of an old woman just out of a beauty parlor, the strands teased and fluffed to disguise balding. If I were a Conjure Man, I'd stomp on the ground above snake dens. The noise would wake the snakes. They'd ignore the cold, break hibernation, slither out, and dance around me like ballerinas. I'd hate to attract the attention of a Duhlak, a robust bird that is part man, part ostrich. Duhlaks live on human flesh. They prefer their meals well-salted and thrived when shipwrecks occurred every day and the bodies of drowned sailors were as common as kelp. Today, Duhlaks are endangered, and since Storrs is a goodly distance from the Atlantic, the chance of a Duhlak's hearing my stomping would be slender. In any case, I'm only a Conjure Man early in the morning. Besides this afternoon I have to drive Vicki to West Hartford to see the eye doctor. Her vision is poor. Uveitis has scarred her right eye, and I am worried.

The Old Oaken Bucket

"How dear to my heart are the scenes of my childhood, / When fond recollection presents them to view! / The orchard, the meadow, the deep-tangled wildwood, / And every loved spot which my infancy knew," Samuel Woodworth reminisced in "The Old Oaken Bucket." "The wide-spreading pond, and the mill which stood by it, / The bridge, and the rock where the cataract fell; / The cot of my father, the dairy-house nigh it, / And e'en the rude bucket which hung in the well— / The old oaken bucket, the iron-bound bucket, / The moss-covered bucket which hung in the well." When "fancy" awakens such memories, the narrator swells with tears "of regret." These tears are, more accurately, tears of loss, and the bucket is a synecdoche, a shard evoking a fragmented and almost vanished past, sentimental and momentarily luxuriant with ponds, wild woods, and fond family members. Once popular as an elementary school recitation and singing assignment, the poem now seems more suited to people my age than to unshaven youth, its shrill voice not broken by decades of living.

My study is a jumble of shards, some in boxes and on window ledges, others buried under dunes of books and papers. Their edges jut out akimbo, and sometimes the objects rise into view like the remnants of a lost culture. Of course they are nothing so romantic as earthenware potsherds and corroded Roman coins. They are my oaken buckets, relics of family living. Near my left hand, partially hidden by paper towels I keep close to absorb tea spills, is a hand magnifying glass that belonged to my father. The handle is six inches long and loose. The glass is four and a half in diameter, and the frame enclosing it five-eighths of an inch tall. The frame is silvery and sturdy, dented by years of use. Father kept the glass on an end table next to an armchair in the corner of his and mother's bedroom. Also on the table were a radio and under the glass usually a book or two. In the evening Father turned on the radio and sat in the chair and read. He listened to classical music. Rarely did he identify a composition. The music was simply a melodic accompaniment to page-turning. As I age, shards make me realize my life is not distinct. It's part of a continuum. At night I read in bed. On the table beside the bed sits a radio. Every night before I start reading, I turn on the radio. For years I've kept it tuned to a Swiss classical music station. Rarely do I recognize a piece. For me, as it was for Father, the music is background, lulling and quiet, rarely intruding into a paragraph and breaking my reading.

  On a shelf to my right is *Poems of Tennyson*, a textbook Father used when he was an undergraduate at Vanderbilt. In black ink on the flyleaf, he wrote "Samuel F. Pickering 359 Kissam Hall 1925." He wrote his name in other places in the book, these always in pencil, with the middle initially expanded to "Francis," and beneath his name, "Carthage, Tennessee, U. S. A." Aside from scribbling his name, he didn't doddle on the pages. He had no artistic ability, an absence I have inherited. On one page he drew three and a half lopsided, five-pointed stars. On another page he drew a series of circles that drifted up and around each other looking like the ridges running over the top shell of a small clam, in other words, like nothing. Above an introductory section entitled "Memoranda" which explained metrics and scansion, he wrote, "Get thee Hence." I can read poems aloud as they are meant to sound, but never have I been able to explain metrics. Like Father, I cannot translate the rhythm of poetry into explanatory prose.

Early in the nineteenth century, Launcelot Langstaff complained in *Salmagundi* that Pegasus had become a mulish animal. He would not budge, Langstaff wrote, "unless he lumbered along, a cartload of quotations and explanations and illustrations at his heels." The *Poems* was almost five hundred pages long, of which one hundred and seventy pages were notes, none of which Father seems to have consulted. Unlike Father I enjoy notes and quotations, especially when I fabricate them. Instead of spending hours digging through books hoping to excavate suitable extracts for a lecture, how much easier and more fun it is to make up quotations. Father was witty, and I suspect that had he become teacher like me, he'd have woven tinselly fabricated quotations through his paragraphs.

The *Poems* were more a windmill and stock tank than a bucket. Many poems Father marked, I quoted unbeknownst in essays, among them, "The Bugle Song," "Tears, Idle Tears," "The Eagle," "The Lotus-Eaters," "Rizpah," "Locksley Hall," "Crossing the Bar," and "Tithonus." Father read "Ulysses" on September 28, 1925. He was seventeen, the right age at which to believe the poem inspirational. I ceased smiting "the sounding furrows" forty years ago. I intend to end in Storrs, Connecticut, not in some forsaken Tartarus "beyond the sunset." For me the "Happy Isles" are cruise-ship stops in the Caribbean, comfortable, pampering places where I can enjoy what has been safely experienced innumerable times. Tom Masson captures my state of mind in his poem "Enough." "I shot a rocket in the air, / It fell to earth, I knew not where / Until next day, with rage profound, / The man it fell on came around. / In less time than it takes to tell, / He showed me where that rocket fell, / And now I do not greatly care / To shoot more rockets in the air."

Tracing Father's markings through the poems made me question my individuality. Of course I am now sixty-five years older than the college boy who read Tennyson. In "Tears, Idle Tears," Father underscored the lines describing tears that rose in the heart after "looking on the happy Autumn-fields, / And thinking of the days that are no more." The lines smack of Woodward's postured nostalgia. In 1925 they probably appealed more to Father's teacher than to Father himself who hadn't lived through two decades. Similarly "Tithonus" must have attracted Father's teacher more than Father. Because literary archaeology has shown me how much my poetic tastes resemble those of Father, I think I can surmise what Father thought after he became "a white hair'd shadow," and could no longer imagine Apollo's singing "while Ilion like a mist rose into towers." Did he, as I do when contemplating the dispiriting illnesses crippling my friends, momentarily envy the "grassy barrows of the happier dead"?

Josh Billings said that most men went through life like rivers "go to the sea, by following the lay of the land." Certainly, the news friends sent me through the years has followed a worn water course. In their twenties, thirties, and deep into their forties, friends wrote about marriages and the doings of children. In their late forties and fifties, they informed me about achievements, at first enthusiastically. However, as time passed, their ebullience became muted and questions about meaning began to appear. In their sixties many devoted much space to writing about summer homes and travel. In their seventies illnesses dodged and not dodged began to craze their pages. Many letters resembled sheets torn from medical textbooks, and at the end of their seventies, most read like accounts sliced from the obituary pages of a newspaper. In "Merlin and the Gleam," Merlin addressed a young mariner. Father circled the last section of the poem in which Merlin urged the sailor to summon his companions and after launching his "vessel" to follow the gleam before it vanished. "After it, follow it," Merlin implored. "Follow The Gleam." The gleam that attracted Father as a college freshman doesn't tempt me. Most gleams are self-generated delusions, and long ago I learned not to follow them or shoot rockets into the air.

    Living a completely reasonable life, however, is a near-death experience, and before crossing the bar and putting out to sea, many people beach their ships on spits of land. Few stray from the mainland of their lives and embrace podomancy or omphalomancy. Still, the taste of bookish folk like me generally changes. They come to prefer low triviality to high seriousness. Instead of naming a feed store for its owners, W. R. Latimer & Sons, wouldn't it be more fructifying, to call it "Sorghum and Gomorrah"? Instead of tramping through "The Hollow Men," I'd rather skip along with "The Ballad of Ameighlia Maireigh," which begins: "Miss Amelia Mary Cholmondely, / When in summer-time she rode, / Did not look one whit less colmondley / Than in winter when she slode." When

I raised the bucket from the depths of the well, along with Father's magnifying glass and a clew of wormy lines from Tennyson's poetry appeared a library of moss-covered books.

In the introduction to *American Essays*, Edward Everett Hale speculated that the "intellectual idling" inherent in essays probably didn't appeal to American readers. The reason, he mused, was because Americans were hard-working, and feeling "the necessity of accomplishing something," didn't have "leisure enough either to write anything of such an idle character as an essay, or to read it." A hundred and twenty years have passed since the appearance of Hale's book, and today the genre is popular. Tastes evolve and bookish habits change. However, what I think primarily responsible for the different perception of the essay is the increased number of elderly readers, weary people who having shouldered burdens imposed upon them by living prefer their late-life reading and their evenings to be light rather than dark and heavy. Unlike "Adolescents of Letters" who want books to be complex and who relentlessly seek answers, "Old Stagers of Letters," men and women of my discriminatory age, find searches for answers and books purporting to parse the human psyche tedious, stem-windingly boring, death on the page, as my friend Josh puts it. In any case I've read warehouses of essays. Moreover, collections of my essays are stables of library fund-raisers. Never does one of my books cost more than a dollar. "A marketing tactic guaranteeing sales and not reflecting any paucity of acclaim," Vicki reassures me.

The first book I pulled out of the bucket was George Ade's *Bang! Bang!* "A Collection of stories intended to recall memories of the nickel library days when boys were supermen and murder a fine art." These stories, Ade, continued, "will mean nothing to juveniles who have been pampered with roadsters and fed on movies—who never heard of Oliver Optic, Horatio Alger, Jr., and Jack Harkaway, to say nothing of Shorty; Silver Star, the Boy Knight; Skinny, the Tin Peddler; and Frank, who invented the mechanical horse. To some of the older people they come as a happy reminder of the days when all of us were ruined by reading books which could not be obtained at the Public Library." Although the book had been in the bucket for almost a hundred years, none of its pages were water-logged and green with algae. The binding was firm, and, although composed of the ingredients of the sugar doughnuts and Wonder Bread of my childhood, the tales were rousing and hadn't lost any of their invigorating effects since being published in the 1890s in the *Chicago Record*.

Two narratives will supply the literarily malnourished with one hundred and twenty-five percent of their daily requirement of vitamins C, D, and E, plus at least one hundred percent of the recommended dosages of fourteen other vitamins. For the aged adult whose bones creak and snap the stories provide a healing two hundred percent of their dose of calcium. But, yes, there is more: the stories are gluten, yeast, and obscenity free. "The Boy Inventor; or The Demon Bicycle and Its Daring Ride" described the travails and successes of Rollo Johnson. After four years of "incessant toil," eight-year-old Rollo invented an electric bicycle accomplishing "what Edison failed to do." In an upcoming race he knew he'd "make the fastest time that has ever been made." Hector Legrand, a bicycle manufacturer and "millionaire capitalist," warned Rollo not to ride in the race or sell the plans of his bike saying, "you will ruin me and mine." On failing to dissuade Rollo, Legrand drew a dagger and sprang at the boy inventor. Rollo built more than bicycles. He stepped back and pressed an electric button connected to a galvanic plate beneath the floor on which Legrand stood. Immediately Legrand shrieked maniacally and fell down quivering.

The next morning after enduring the taunts of Hooper, the race favorite, Rollo won the race by twenty lengths. As befits a boy hero, Rollo had a taste for the dramatic. At the quarter mile post, he was ten lengths behind. At the half mile he appeared "hopelessly beaten." But then he touched a button, and the bicycle "shot forward like a flash of lightning." Villains are noted more for primitive vitality than craft. While Rollo was racing, some men broke into his mother's house and stole the plans for his bicycle. "I will follow the thieves to the world's end," Rollo later told his tearful mother before he mounted his "demon bicycle" and "rode away like the wind." In another part of the city near the murky Chicago River, Legrand and four swarthy men sat in a basement studying the plans. Suddenly a blinding flash knocked them out of their chairs. Rollo had turned the "the full force of his automo-battery" upon them. He grabbed the plans, but the gang recovered quickly, and a dozen bullets whizzed by him as he escaped on his bicycle. He raced down a street that ended at the edge of the river. "What was he to do?" the story asked. Seeing him near the river, the gang emitted "yells of triumph." In ruinous boyhood reading, heroes always win out. Rollo knew that capture meant certain death so again he pressed an electric button and raising his front wheel shot across the river. Legrand vanished never to be seen again. Afterward the police rounded up his henchmen and sent them to prison for life. "Our hero," the tale concluded, "received a million dollars for his invention and achieved just fame, but he did not relinquish his study, and every day he may be seen in his workshop, inventing some useful article for the betterment of mankind."

Perhaps more satisfactory because it appealed to wholesome American xenophobia was "The Boy Champion; or America's Fair Name Defended." "No," George Webster shouted at the beginning of the story, refusing the hundred thousand dollars Mortimer Blake offered him to throw an international boxing match. As tears flooded his eyes, George said, "I have told you that I would not engage in this pugilistic encounter were it not for the fact I desire to provide for my dear mother and my sister Irene and protect the glorious Stars and Stripes." The refusal so infuriated Blake that he pulled out a pistol and shot George twice in the chest. "The reader," the narrator then remarked, "has no doubt recognized ere this the Chicago boy champion, George Webster, who at the age of thirteen had made for himself a reputation on both sides of the Atlantic and had vanquished a score of valiant fighters."

George was a never-say-die and never-stop-thinking boy. To the meeting with Blake he wore a bullet-proof jacket. In the meantime muttering "the girl shall be mine," Vincent Edgerton, one of Blake's associates, planned to abduct George's sister Irene. He instructed the Water Rat, "a bearded ruffian whose hideous features were an index to his depraved soul," to poison George's food. The boy will lose the fight. His family will be ruined, and "I can claim Irene as my own," Edgerton said. After surviving the attempted murder, George told his trainer Reddy Muldoon, "Our enemies are at work. The British government has its emissaries in our midst, and they will employ every means to accomplish their devilish purpose." "Let us not fear. The American people are with us," Muldoon responded. George was a right-feeling, spontaneous boy not reluctant to reveal his emotions, and with a "teardrop glistening in his eye," he told Muldoon, "I will defend the glorious star-spangled banner with my life." Suddenly there was a terrific explosion; the floor on which he and Muldoon stood shattered into "a million fragments." The walls of the building collapsed, and the ceiling "rocked with a fearful crash." As the ceiling was falling, George leaped through the doorway "dragging his faithful trainer behind him." Outside the building an old man shouted, "three cheers for the boy champion," and a stranger handed him a note that said Irene was missing.

"We must be alert," George said. Actually, Irene wasn't missing. As befitted a relative of George, Irene was similarly alert. In a palatial hotel in a magnificent apartment, two fashionable dressed men sat at marble table drinking champagne. One was Lord Romney, the other Guy Beresford, a secret agent of the British government. On Blake's appearing and saying he had failed to eliminate George, Lord Romney exclaimed angrily, "Should this American youth win, the British government will be disgraced before the world." Saying that he had received a message from the Prime Minister demanding that George "must be put out of the way at all hazards," Romney declared that it was essential that George be drugged and "carried away." Shouting "cowards," "a beautiful young girl in pure white, with heavy chestnut curls falling about her shoulders" stepped out from behind a hanging curtain. In each hand she held a "gleaming pistol." With eyes blazing and her lips curled in scorn, she said, "I have heard your nefarious plotting ... But your dastardly schemes will never succeed. George Webster is an American, and the American people will support him in his endeavor to protect the glorious Stars and Stripes, even as their forefathers protected our proud flag at Bunker Hill."

Irene was no domestic Betsy Ross content to sit at home and sew the American flag. She resembled Catherine Barry, the heroine of the Battle of Cowpens. As George sat mulling his fight with Tug Smith who outweighed him by eighty pounds and was celebrated as "the greatest fighter that ever came from England," Irene burst into the room, saying that she had just shot two men preventing them from poisoning George's food. The fight itself was anti-climactic. Around his waist George wore a sash decorated with stars and stripes, a talisman more inspiriting and efficacious than any voodoo juju. Five times George dodged death-dealing blows. Then when Smith paused, George leaped into the air and smashed Smith on the chin, ending the fight, after which he declared that he was proud the championship remained in America. Before he left the building, four men passed by, carrying the body of Lord Romney who died of a broken heart. The police captured Vincent Edgerton who, George said, "will trouble us no more." In the final scene George "clad in a rich dressing gown" sat in his beautiful home between his dear mother and darling sister. He was reading telegrams congratulating him on his glorious victory, among them one written by President McKinley. "Promise me that you will never again engage in a pugilistic contest," the hero's mother said, stroking his hair. "I promise mother," he replied tenderly. "I promise that I will not do so, except in defense of the dear old Stars and Stripes." In *Bang! Bang!* boys were boys, and girls were girls. They hadn't been schooled into cautious respectability. Before I deteriorated into being a good student, such stories were my bedtime companions.

Years ago in the basement of the university library, I discovered John Warner Barber's *Connecticut Historical Collections*, the initial edition of which appeared in 1836. Barber lived in New Haven and produced books illustrated with wood and steel engravings. For *Collections* he traveled Connecticut amassing facts and anecdotes and sketching scenes from sundry towns. In the middle of the print of Mansfield appeared a church, the only Presbyterian church, Barber thought, in Connecticut. Today the church is Congregational. The building has been replaced, but its descendant has the same tall steeple and stands on the same corner of land in Storrs, now the intersection of the North Eagleville Road and Route 195. In the background looms Horsebarn Hill. The hill appears almost unchanged today. It rises in the same slow inviting curve. Around its edges trees grow in the places where they have grown for one hundred and eight-five years. Because a late spring snow storm prevented Vicki and me from taking her to St. George's Episcopal Church in Nashville, Eliza was christened in Storrs at the Congregational Church. I cannot explain why the heart leaps higher than the mind when a person unexpectedly discovers his footprints or the footprints of others whom he has followed. But seeing the print depicting the church and Horsebarn Hill raised my spirits. It made me feel that I belonged, and momentarily, my life seemed less erasable. Enforcing the feeling was the second book in the bucket, Barber's *Christian Similitudes*

"Illustrated by a Series of Emblematic Engravings." The book contained some forty-five emblems, among them, "Heathenism," "Faith, Hope, and Love," "The Pardoned Sinner," "The Backslider," "The Sanctified Christian," and "The Synagogue of Satan." "The gentle sisters" Fear and Hope held hands as they traveled toward heaven, Fear carrying a shield, Hope an anchor. Before a man standing atop the steps—Prayer, Hope, and Faith—stretched "The Spiritual Telegraph," its line mounted on poles and climbing hills through dark clouds into the light. In "The Memory of Wickedness," a man slumped beside a desk, his right elbow on the desktop, his hand pressed against his cheek. His brow was furrowed, and he looked anguished. Above him circled vignettes of memory: his scorning his mother's instruction, fighting and quarrelling, and driving the poor and needy from his presence. Several vignettes were hazy and subject to interpretation. "Perhaps in addition to other crimes and misdemeanors," Barber suggested, he "betrayed female innocence by false promises."

The emblems resembled playful drawings that have long appeared in newspapers, puzzle books, and on table mats in diners. Hidden in these illustrations amid tangles of lines and rockpiles of circles are zoos of animals—not good deeds and sins but gamesome creatures meant to delight young explorers. Although my favorite emblem in *Similitudes* "The Unregenerate Heart" at first looked like a cartoon drawn for a child, it was a corral of iconographic creatures, all thrusting through the valves of the heart. The fallen heart like fallen Babylon, Barber wrote, was the habitation of devils, "the hole of every foul spirit, and a cage of every unclean and hateful bird." At the aorta a "flaunting peacock" spread its tail. Nearby at folly, an ape smiled stupidly. Twisting out of the right atrium a serpent spread its deceitful jaws. A mole clung to the left atrium, its blindness akin to the darkness of the soul. A goat grinned licentiously, and ill will, anger, and revenge marked the face of a tiger. While a hyena appeared murderous, a pig was gluttonous, its snout enlarged and snuffling. A crocodile looked out of the left ventricle. "Fraud aptly shows the weeping crocodile," Barber warned, "which draws its victim by its piteous wile." A servile toad squatted, its feet digging into the right ventricle of the heart. The toad gets its living close to the ground, Barber wrote, and thereby was known for "a covetous and earthly-minded disposition." A bat clung to the superior vena cava. The bat represented guilt. It partakes partly "of the nature of a beast, and partly that of a bird," Barber said. "It seeks obscurity and generally moves or flies about during the shades of night, and appears to have a peculiar aversion to the light of the sun."

When an oaken bucket is stored in a barn, its contents evaporate and disappear from dry memory. However the moment a bucket is hauled wet and splashing out of the past, the contents are familiar. Hoisting matters from depths other than from the past is impossible. Buckets are roped to the puller's mind. Mary Sparkes Wheeler wrote the final book in the bucket, *As It Is In Heaven* "By One of the Redeemed" published in 1906. Wheeler was a great reader. She wrote poems and hymns, was active in the Temperance Movement and the Women's Foreign Missionary Society and was an admired speaker. She had seven children, five of whom didn't survive childhood, a melancholy fact that soaks her pages. Finding her book in the bucket reflected my interest in religion and evangelical writings. I have often written about ruinous boys' books. My affection for them did not end with childhood but still continues. Years ago I wrote about emblems, but I have written more about religious narratives than any other genre. For fifty years I've rummaged the dusty corners of libraries much as I did attics and basements when I was a boy, the grimier the shelves the more fun I had. Only small-minded people demand consistency. Although not a believer, rarely did I criticize religious books harshly. They intrigued me, and I marveled at and appreciated the stories that enlivened their pages.

Wheeler dedicated her book to "The Vast Numbers of Those Whose Departed Friends Closed Their Eyes in Death To Awaken in The Beautiful Morning." The narrator became, in effect, one of those people. She was married for five years, but after being soaked in a rain storm, her husband caught pneumonia and died. "The sun of my life went down. All was darkness save the halo of light that encircled the life of my precious daughter," she said, speaking of her child Edith. Not long after her husband's death, the narrator herself became ill and died. When she awoke from that final sleep, she heard enchanting music. Her vision was clearer, and her intellect keener. She saw majestic trees and wondrous flowers. Beautiful birds sang marvelous songs. Flowing near her was a crystalline river "with myriads of the purest lilies floating on its surface." Shortly thereafter she met her husband. "My darling one, Welcome Home. Good Morning!" he said, "Death can no more take me from your fond embrace." They joined hands and together became guides escorting readers on a tour of heaven. They seasoned their conversation with telling sermons and instructive anecdotes. They talked about B who lived a happy, joyous life because he "enjoyed the consciousness of his acceptance with God." B had a friend who was pure and noble but occasionally "troubled with doubts." Early one morning as the friend worked in a field, he heard the fluttering of pinions and "an overwhelming power overcame him." He rushed to B's house and discovered B had unexpectantly died. "How did you hear of it?" B's wife asked. "I knew it," the man replied, "for I heard the rustle of the angels' wings as they came for him."

Not long afterward the redeemed couple traveled to the town in which they had lived. They stopped outside a house in which the window blinds were shut and the front door hung with crape. "Who among my friends has died since I went away?" the redeemed wife asked. The couple did not enter the house through the door. "The barriers of earth were no longer barriers to us," the wife explained. "We could glide through wall or ceiling as easily as through air." Inside the house beautiful flowers surrounded a coffin. "Let us look at the sleeper in the casket," the husband said. "To my astonishment," the wife said, I saw "myself lying there amid the flowers." Among the sorrow-stricken mourners were her friends and neighbors and saddest of all her beloved Edith. Attending my own funeral does not appeal to me, and I have repeatedly told Vicki that I don't want a funeral. But if she ignores my wish then I'd like my cold meat to heat up for just a moment, long enough for me to kick aside the lid of my bone box and scare the hell out of everyone in the church—hell in this sense measuring excitement and not having any theological implication.

Such a fright would not be reformative. It wouldn't purge sin, purify, and guarantee mourners seats in the first class compartment on the streamliner racing toward Beulah Land. But my popping up suddenly, gas wheezing, feet dancing, head bobbling, and rigor mortis bending me like a folding chair might cause a few folks to shout, "Save Me Jesus." I wonder how long the others would remain in their pews when a toad bounded out of my throat and turned my tongue into a lily pad. I suspect The Spirit would possess them, and they'd be more animated than Wheeler's redeemed couple. Instead of gliding silently between walls, they'd bulldoze their ways outside smashing windows and sheet rock, all the while weeping, moaning, and gnashing their dentures. An account of these doings surely would make angels clap their wings. Maybe the heavenly gang would belt down a few tumblers of copper-still eggnog and play a little old time religion on their harps, stirring pieces like "Faith of Our Fathers" and "Marching to Zion." My corpse would like to hear "Shall We Gather at the River" or a spiritual like "Going to Shout All Over God's Heaven," maybe even a temperance song like "Look Not Upon the Wine" or "Hurrah for Sparkling Water." Once the "Gospel Train" starts down my pages, its music clacking across lines, I don't want to get off. If all The Good Mornings were so inspiring, I wouldn't fritter away my casket time terrifying mourners. I'd head up to the sun faster than a dew drop, as Wheeler wrote describing the death of a little baby.

In Wheeler's heaven, the Holy Book was an anthology of inspirational didactic stories. I recalled a tale once told to me, the narrator recollected "of a Russian soldier one piercing cold night, who paced between one sentry box and another. A poor working man, moved with pity, took off his coat and lent it to the soldier to keep him warm, adding that he would soon reach home, while the soldier would be exposed out of doors for the night." Unfortunately the cold was so intense that the soldier died. Sometime afterward as the poor man lay on his deathbed, Jesus visited him in a dream. "You have got my coat," the poor man said. "Yes," Jesus answered. "It is the coat you lent to me that cold night when I was on duty and you passed by. 'I was naked and you clothed me.'"

In heaven, the narrator met her sister Elsie who died as a child. Because the "earthly vocabulary is empty and meaningless," she had difficulty describing her sister. Elsie wore a white robe "like no white on earth." Spangling the robe were gems which reflected the light of heaven. Elsie was leading a children's choir. I wanted to know what they were singing, "Blessed Assurance," "Down to the River to Pray," or maybe "In the Garden," gospel songs that Wayfaring Strangers know but which are not high on the local Hit Parade. Despite the failings of sin-stained words, the narrator attempted to describe a young chorister. "There was nothing with which the blessed babe, or child, could be compared," she said apologetically. "It seemed to be about three feet high. Its wings, which were long and most beautiful, were tinged with all the colors of the rainbow. Its dress seemed to be of the whitest silk, covered with the softest white down. The driven snow could not exceed it for whiteness or purity. Its face was all radiant with glory." The narrator said she "gazed and gazed upon this heavenly child," adding that if she had to return to earth, she'd love to take the child and show it to bereaved mothers. "I think when they see it, they will never shed another tear over their children when they die."

In part the narrator experienced a family reunion. Unlike earthly gatherings in which family members migrate from sundry towns and countries, I assume shades of the saved travel from different epochs. At a heavenly reunion recognizing kin would be difficult. On such occasions everybody would appear in the same fraternal dress. Each person would wear a white robe and wouldn't wear clothes fashionable in the epochs in which they died, that is, no codpieces or ruffles, no doublets or broad-brimmed hats. Making recognition more difficult would be that none of the inhabitants of heaven would seem old. Wrinkles vanish, the narrator noticed, adding that there were no tottering limbs, "no dull eyes or heavy ears, no gray hair, and everyone was "clothed in rigorous strength and beauty." Present among the sanctified whom the narrator recognized immediately was Auntie "a colored woman remarkable no less for her ability as a cook, than for her fidelity to God and her church." Auntie was among a group of celestial spirits singing hymns. Like all her fellow spirits she was "white as the light," and instead of a turban she wore a crown of glory. Her pantry days were long behind her. Now she was a servant of the Lord, and instead of being careworn, her countenance was "blissful and serene."

I confess that I am not ready for the Lord to "fill my cup," as the gospel song implores. I prefer Coca-Cola to milk and honey, and ichor doesn't agree with my arteries and gives me arrhythmia. My muscles have shrunk like leeches out of water, but I can still push myself out of bed in the morning without the help of the Everlasting Arms. Moreover, I can't imagine being satisfied by a holiness diet of eternal truths even if seasoned with the "sweet will of God." At family reunions I like variety. Hold the Bread of Life and serve me buttermilk biscuits and Grandma's "divine" four-layer chocolate cake. Of course, good cornbread is also heavenly, not something I've tasted since moving to the Northeast.

At reunions in The Kingdom no disreputable Uncle Jeb entertains the family by tripping the heavy alcoholic toe and almost drowning in "the sauce," and the reputation of Cousin Alice Stained Gown is brighter, and duller, than the Milky Way, the "Gateway to Heaven." Backbiting and relatives squabbling about wills delight me. Salvation is probably nice, but I need to prepare a little more before Abraham rings the curtain down. At this moment I agree with the poet who said sanctification "ain't all." Of course for the narrator it was everything. At the end of her walkabout, she was "dumb with delight" to learn that her daughter Edith was coming. Meeting her father, mother, sister, and brother transported her with joy. But declaring that to clasp her child in "the Kingdom" would be the dearest joy of all, she hurried to prepare a room for her daughter's reception. But as could be expected, angels had already strewn the room with lilies, and "there white-robed and garlanded" stood Edith. She and Edith were too filled with love to speak. Wordlessly, Edith "pillowed" her head on her mother's bosom, and her father wrapped his arms around them. "When at length we lifted our faces," the wife recounted. The air was filled with music, and we saw "encircling us, without and within, our mansion, a multitude of redeemed ones, many of whom we had known and loved on earth, who with angelic spirits were rejoicing with us." Together, the narrator concluded, we lifted "our hearts in a song of adoration to him who hath given us when we awake in his likeness, to enter with Him into THE LIFE ETERNAL."

Life, Sir William Temple said, "is like wine; he who would drink it pure, must not drain it to the dregs." Similarly, the last cups of water at the bottom of buckets are gravelly. All family genealogies are apocryphal. Story tellers uncomplicate lives and force living into understandable narratives with beginnings, middles, and ends. People overly conscious of reputation prune branches and lop limbs off family trees. The trunks that remain resemble posts at the ends of picket fences: straight and ostensibly firm, smooth, all knots planed off, and easily white-washable. In the dregs beneath *As It Is In Heaven* lay a sheaf of newspaper articles published in 1875 and 1881 describing life as it was on earth. A stranger whose hobby was studying gunfights on town squares sent me the papers. I know much about William Pickering, the father of my grandfather Sam Pickering. In 1861 when he was seventeen he left Ohio University and enlisted in the 18th Ohio Infantry. I know the battles in which he fought. I have letters he wrote and have seen orders he signed. Mounted on the wall in the television room is box containing his pistol, a diary he kept, and the pen with which General Mitchener signed his commission after Stones River. On a shelf in the study is *The Works of Lord Byron in Verse and Prose* given to him by his father before the war and later used by my father at Vanderbilt in 1929 his senior year. In 1865 at the end of the war he married Eliza McClarin from Carthage, Tennessee. After a sojourn in Athens, Ohio, the couple returned to and spent the rest of their lives in Carthage. I know many things about him: his role in founding the Methodist Sunday School and running as a Republican against Cordell Hull for Congress. If a person can really be known, he is a known character: admirable, admired, and loved. Often my father and grandfather talked about him fondly and respectfully.

Sam Pickering, my grandfather, married Francis Griffin. I know much about her mother Nannie Brown. Two years before the war she graduated from a small college in Tennessee. She was valedictorian, and I have the address she gave at graduation. In my study are six small books from her library. Adorning the titlepage of each is a fanciful, calligraphic drawing of her name. The drawings are also poetic. Vines twine around stems. Birds soar over shoulders, and bouquets of flowers hang from ascenders and swing through counters. Fittingly the volumes themselves are collections of poetry: works by Milton and Wordsworth, Lydia Sigourney and Felicia Hemans, then Scott's *The Lady of The Lake* and Moore's *Lalla Rookh*. Nannie Brown was gentle and cultivated and taught school. In a box in the attic are letters written by her suitors. With the exception of those written by Daniel F. Griffin, the man she married, the letters are courtly and dull. Griffin's school was the war. In 1861 he joined the 36th Regiment of the Georgia Infantry. He was fifteen years old. He fought until 1864 when he was badly wounded in Atlanta on July 22. At the end of September, he was in a hospital in Columbus. Unlike William Pickering, Griffin was rarely mentioned when I was growing up. Grandma Pickering, his daughter, never said his name. Somehow, I learned that his friends called him "Bud" and that during war he was a sergeant and a martinet. As befitting his harsh education, Griffin's letters were forceful and direct. I do not know what led Griffin to Franklin, Tennessee and Williamson County. On one occasion he returned to Georgia and wrote Nannie saying that he'd seen the man who shot him but his love for her prevented him from putting a bullet in the man's head. I know nothing more about the incident or about the possibility of similar incidents. For a time Griffin left Franklin and went to Texas. I didn't know why until I scraped the bottom of the bucket. I had a stack of letters he wrote from Texas to Nannie in the late 1870s, but one night Father threw them away. I assumed that after having a drink Father had gone on a white-washing the family spree and removed the letters from the top shelf of my bedroom closet. Decades ago, I asked Father about Griffin explaining that I planned to write about a little about him "to balance Union with Confederate." "You don't want to know about him," Father replied, ending the conversation.

Until I received the clippings, I knew little more than that Griffin died after returning from Texas and that Nannie Brown's siblings in Franklin and Bellevue, Tennessee, helped raise my grandmother. The clippings were the stuff of a novel, not suitable for pretensions to gentility and to an idling essayistic identity, or so Father may have thought. "Bloody Work in Franklin" read the headline atop an article which appeared on October 22, 1875 in the Nashville paper *The Tennessean*. In smaller type a secondary headline elaborated, saying, "Col. John L. House shot to Pieces by The Recorder and Marshall of the Town." A day later the *Memphis Daily Appeal* published a similar article under the caption "Recorder and Town Marshall in a Bad Box—A Chance for Hemp Stretching." House had "made a gallant soldier" and had been Colonel of the First Tennessee Regiment, one account stated. I first ran across him in Samuel Watkins's description of the Battle of Nashville in *Co Atych*. At the time House was a Lieutenant-Colonel and was on Shy's Hill with William Shy. Unlike Shy, House survived. He was outspoken and hot tempered, but he was a leader.

Some historians attribute much of the responsibility of the race riot in Franklin in 1867 to House. Causes of the riot were mixed although its essential ingredient was race. Members of the "Colored" Union League advocated civil rights, supported the Republican party, and agitated for the enfranchisement of former slaves and black Union soldiers. Opposing the League when its members marched through Franklin beating drums was a group of disenfranchised Confederate veterans and conservative whites, albeit some former slaves were in their ranks. Similarly a few whites supported the League. The Conservatives gathered outside House's home, reportedly under his command, and a Conservative seems to have fired the first shot. The number of people killed wasn't high though one writer dubbed the fracas a "Carnival of Blood." The Conservatives were better armed than members of the League, and a reporter noted that twenty-seven "colored men" whose wounds were dressed by Dr. D. B. Cliff were shot in the back or "in the back part of the limbs." Over time historical facts often become hearsay. One writer said that the Williamson County chapter of the Ku Klux Klan was founded in House's home. If the report is accurate, and it may not be, it serves to make House less appealing to the present. In his time he was popular, and the *Public Ledger* published in Memphis said he was "known all over the state as a gallant gentleman." He was a Mason, a Democrat, "a prominent candidate for Comptroller in 1873," and his "funeral was one of the largest ever in Franklin."

    The other major actor in the drama on the Franklin town square was my great-grandfather, "one Griffin" as papers generally referred to him. City Marshall and "proprietor of a saloon," he "was spoken of as a man of cool, undaunted courage." Griffin and House, a witness to the shooting recounted, "had, for some time past shown a want of appreciation of each other that amounted to positive coolness." One account of the gunfight accused Griffin of using his office "to gratify personal feeling." Certainly, Griffin appears quarrelsome, but I wonder if their stature in the war contributed to their antipathy. In the conclusion to *Co. Atych* Samuel Watkins wrote that the "private soldier fought and starved and died for naught." House was a celebrated officer, and Griffin an anonymous private when he enlisted and a sergeant when he was wounded. Incidentally, House was also present at the Battle of Atlanta commanding the First Tennessee Regiment.

Perhaps, however, the mutual dislike only reflected a difference in the local perception of class, Griffin being from Georgia, not Tennessee, something that would have rankled my relative. Defining "gentleman" is always chancy, but in contrast to House no account of the shooting lauded Griffin as a gentleman. I, as Griffin's great-grandson, think most social gradations specious, be they high or low, based on ephemeral achievement or failure or, as they so often are, pretension and self-generated acclaim. Throughout my life stiff knees have prevented me from genuflecting, thankfully something a university teacher rarely must do. Poor manners nettle me, but the only thing I ever fired were hot words, and years ago my pen cooled and I disarmed my sentences.

Two other players appeared in the drama. The more important was W. M. Allison, the town recorder who actually may have fired the shot that killed House. Newspapers noted that Allison was an attorney and an elder in the Methodist Church but did not give his

Christian name. Also on stage was House's only son Mansfield, known as Manse. He was praised for his "good traits" and having the "highest character," his "devoted love for his father" being one of its "noblest points." Mansfield's appearance was brief. Griffin shot him as soon after he stepped into the square. He then vanished into the wings as friends quickly transported him five miles out of town and refused to inform him about his father's death. One paper said his wound was mortal. Griffin's bullet struck him in the pelvis "just below the abdomen" and ranged around finally lodging against the hip bone paralyzing one leg. Although serious, young House had "chances" to survive, one writer said, among "which is the weather."

The drama on the square smacked of Elizabeth revenge tragedy. Certainly it was complicated and bloody. The first act occurred at ten o'clock the previous night in Butler's Saloon. House had a "drinking problem" and during the course of the evening he cursed Dr. Shy "very loudly." "It was stated," a report recounted, "that Col. House had told Blackhawk Nichol that Griffin had loaned Dr. Shy [Louis Shy the brother of Colonel William Shy killed at the Battle of Nashville] the shotgun to shoot Jim Neely some time ago." Accompanied by Allison, Griffin then approached House "to see" about it. After he called House a damned rascal, and House retorted that he was a damned liar, a scuffle broke out. Allison supposedly rushed between the men and with a stick pushed House back. Griffin then leaned over Allison's shoulder and hit House on the head with a mace "cutting a gash one and a half inches and to the bone." Friendship seems to have determined the testimony of bystanders. House's friends said Allison hit House with his stick; Allison's, that he just lay the stick against House's chest.

From here on events became complicated but murderous. While Dr. Gentry was treating House's head in the back of Carothers Store, Allison stepped through the door asking for Judge Cook and holding a pistol. On being recognized by House, Allison left. The next day House went to Allison's office, and saying that the affair should be settled then and there, invited him into the street. Shortly afterward House and Griffin met, and matters seemed to be dying down although House berated Griffin for hitting him with the mace and not doing right by him. Allison cursed Dr. Shy and accused him of causing the trouble. But then he suggested to Griffin that he arrest House. Griffin agreed to do so, but worried that Manse House might shoot him, he delegated Allison to keep an eye on Manse. Carrying a large navy pistol and the mace, Griffin approached House "in a rapid gait." He grabbed House's lapel and jerked him forward. House cursed and said he would accompany Griffin, but he "would not be forced or dragged." As they started into the street, Manse House appeared at the door of Carothers store. In his hand was a pistol. Griffin asked Manse if "he intended to draw his pistol on him, at the same time placing his weapon over Col. House's shoulder" and aiming at Manse. Manse pointed his pistol at the ground and said he didn't intend to shoot whereupon House declared he would and "commenced drawing his pistol." Griffin then stepped back and shot House in the groin area. "It is claimed by many," the report from the inquest stated, that House did not draw his pistol until after Griffin shot him. Many others testified that House "presented his pistol at Griffin and snapped it." They said House aimed his pistol at Griffin's chest and would have killed him had the pistol not misfired. As he "flanked around in Main Street," House continued to snap his pistol. The caps failed to explode and bystanders heard him say, "oh, pshaw." Until his pistol also misfired Griffin continue to shoot, hitting House three more times.

After Griffin's initial shot, Manse ran into the street, and Griffin "turned his revolver loose" hitting Manse once. Manse then tumbled over and said, "stop, Griffin, stop, don't shoot no more." Friends took Mansfield from the street, and one offered him a shot gun. Mansfield said he was too hurt to use it, so the friend, perhaps Fount Pritchett, raced into the crowd and tried to shoot Griffin. The gun misfired whereupon another person knocked it aside. House himself had nearly crossed Main Street when Allison wearing a silk hat shot at him from the corner of Cayce's Store. Although hit, House continued to snap his pistol at Griffin. Allison fired again, and House fell back "a corpse." Saying "it was an outrage for a man to shoot from behind a corner," a man near Allison "jerked up a big rock" and chased him away. "After Col. House fell," one of the observers testified, "my attention was directed to a wagon and team about to run over the body, and I took hold of the horses and backed them out of the way."

For the record House was shot five times: near the hip, in the groin, in the right arm, the right shoulder, and on the right side striking a bone and "dancing around so to speak" and ending in the right buttock. The most serious and probably the fatal wound resulted from Allison's shot. It entered House's body from the right side between the sixth and seventh ribs, passing through his lungs, and "completely penetrating his body." The coroner's jury found the killing "wholly unjustified" and indicted Allison and Griffin for murder. Bond was set at six thousand dollars. Nannie Brown's brothers, Enoch, James, Innis, and other relatives put up the money. Later, Griffin was acquitted and left Franklin for the cooler climate of sweltering Texas. The acquittal didn't end the drama completely. A bloodstained denouement remained to be acted when Griffin returned to Tennessee. Among the papers was a short piece published in the *Pulaski Citizen* on February 10, 1881. "D. F. Griffin, the man who so ruthlessly murdered Col. House on the streets of Franklin five years ago, was himself killed in a billiard saloon in Franklin last Thursday night by John Wells, Jr. Wells is the brother of Ed Wells, once conductor on our road, and acted in self-defense. Griffin received the same number of wounds that he inflicted upon Col. House and was killed within fifty feet of the spot where House fell. He was a desperate man and met the fate of all such, yet to his friends he was generous and unstinted in kindness to his family." Stories are paradoxical. They end but don't end. Did the killing simply result from a quarrel or was it motivated by revenge or by something else, familial anger or jealousy?

    The notice seemed a reprinting of a paragraph which appeared on February 4 in the *Nashville Banner*. The old bucket did not contain that paper. Among other papers, however, was a rejoinder written by Gerald Griffin, Daniel's brother in Cartersville, Georgia. He criticized "the hasty penning for publication" of the description of his brother's shooting "long in advance of any investigation" by a court. Not only was the piece "an outrage upon private rights and the laws of the land" but it should be "deplored by all good citizens" for its evil and unjust tendencies. Until both sides were heard from, he wrote, no one outside "that billiard room" knows or can know "what occurred immediately preceding and during the fatal shooting." He said he was addressing "good citizens" in the name of Justice and on behalf "of the sorrowing hearts of the relatives and friends of my brother who was most cruelly and unmercifully shot while in a defenseless position." The tone was rigid and hard, yet gentle and soft. A person reads about family in hopes of discovering himself. Gerald seem to be the sort of person I'd like for a relative, if one can judge a person by his prose. People in Williamson county "and elsewhere" who knew Daniel, he said, recognized that he "was as magnanimous as he was brave." "Of his enemies and who has them not," Gerald said, Daniel "would scorn to entertain even the thought of taking advantage. He was as generous to a foe as he was as kind and loving to his friends."

Gerald said that the accusation that his brother was often in personal difficulties and had been shot several times since the war was "destitute of even the semblance of truth." The only such difficulty was "the lamentable occurrences a few years since in this place" [Franklin]. Gerald ended with a ringing tribute to his brother or as the ancient platitude says, "he who preaches last preaches best." Daniel, Gerald wrote, "was severely wounded during the war while honorably engaged at the front fighting the invaders of his country. When only a stripling about fifteen years of age, he volunteered his services to the Southern Confederacy and served her zealously to the close of the war, making an enviable reputation for gallantry upon the battlefields of his country. In him there was no guile, no deceit. He was brave, manly, straightforward in all his actions. He never imposed himself upon his fellow man, nor would suffer himself nor any of his to be imposed upon, when in his power to avert it."

At its best, Hazlitt wrote, the essay portrays the mixed nature of human affairs. It examines the world of men and women and holding the mirror up to nature "records their actions, assigns their motives, exhibits their whims, characterizes their pursuits in all their singular and endless variety, ridicules their absurdities" and "exposes their inconsistencies." Words not facts create truths, and lies. History is soluble like limestone. Showers of words seep through the rock and create runnels that alter appearance and reality. Moreover like a mirror even immediate truths do not capture events accurately. Images are reversed. The surfaces of mirrors and events tarnish and spot. Silvering falls away, and details are distorted often becoming convex or concave.

I don't know what to conclude about Daniel Griffin. Life is infinitely fuller and more complicated than any paragraphs I might write. In the once-upon-a-time world, eye drops made from spring water and the ashes of owls' eyes cleared one's visions, both the outer focused on the exterior world and the inner, that is, the understanding. CVS sells aviaries of eye drops, among others, Systane, Visine, Rohto, and Optimum Eyes, this last all-natural and made from castor oil. However, the pharmacy does not peddle drops manufactured from the oculi of feathered members of the Tytonidae and Strigidae tribes. In the deep past owls were flying pharmacopeias. Burning their feet and mixing the embers with water and plumbago blossoms produced a contraceptive tonic against snakebite. Although the bites of bullets are often not as sharp and venomous as those of serpents, I suspect that not even a case of tonic could have defanged the violence in Franklin.

"You're not your own great-grandpa," Vicki said emending Lonzo and Oscar's novelty song, "I'm My Own Grandpa." "You don't hold grudges, and slights shrivel and drop out of your mind quicker than slugs sprinkled with salt. Words are the only bullets you fire. Sometimes sentences bang, but because the bullets are blanks and you don't aim at actual people, they are only irritating noise." "You mean I'm not a hot shot, packing paragraphs primed with the goods?" I replied. "A touch of the goods, but none of the bads," Vicki said. Shunting Vicki's disarming opinion of me as a literary gunslinger onto a siding, Wheeler was wrong when she wrote that life was eternal. Lives are as short-lived as allegory. When historical accounts age, they are often momentarily alluring turning yellow and blue like rotting flesh. They catch the eye, but one should not dig into them deeply as their poison might seep into the mind. Better to use one's shovel in the present. A foot of snow fell last night, and today the driveway, not the past, will be the only thing I'll dig into. Nevertheless, before bundling up and heading outside, I must admit that I wouldn't have admired Colonel House. He had too much of Barber's hyena and tiger in his character, his preening peacock pride, and if he and my great-grandfather met in Wheeler's heaven, they would wear scarlet rather than white robes. All the trees would be yews; turkey buzzards the only birds singing, and the "green sward" dry and brown. News of Griffin's death did not make his family "dumb with delight" or fill his wife and children with the "silent heaven of love." When Daniel Griffin died, he was thirty-six. My grandmother was two years old.

On the very bottom of the old bucket plugging a slow leak lay a poem, not verses by Tennyson, but "Dear Father, Look Up" by Orpheus C. Kerr, a contemporary of George Ade. A smidgen of violence appears in the poem, but like that in *Bang! Bang!* it is cartoonish. Light-hearted, the poem is just the panacea to soothe one's mood after he has swallowed the grit of family story. On returning home after working in a field, Woolworth's narrator called the oaken bucket brimming with water "the source of an exquisite treasure." Kerr's poem is also a treasure, refreshing and raising one's spirits—a cheerful, small-tent invigorator stronger than a platter of goats' testicles, just the "ticket" to buck a fellow up before he shovels snow.

> Dear Father, look up,
> Away from the cup,
> And tell me what aileth Ma's forehead.
> It's all black and blue;
> O, what could she do
> To cause a contusion so horrid?
>
> Your mother, Jane Ann.
> A newspaper man
> Admired till I warn'd her she'd catch it;
> Like Washington, I
> Cannot tell a lie—
> I did it with my little hatchet.

Likeness

In 1801, Coleridge observed that "In natural objects we feel ourselves, or think of ourselves, only by *likenesses*, among men, too often by *differences*. Hence the soothing love-kindling effect of rural nature—-the bad passions of human societies. And why is difference linked with hatred?" Home is not where a person grows up, but where he recognizes the birds and trees, flowers, and animals that wander the night and wear trails through wood and yard. In "The Pleasures of Hope," Thomas Campbell speculated about the appeal of remote mountains to the "musing eye," asking, "Why do those cliffs of shadowy tint appear / More sweet than all the landscape smiling near?" Campbell was a Romantic. The meticulously representational and the closely observed did not attract him as strongly as things dimly perceived. These last awakened the imagination and invited the viewer, in Wordsworth's phrase, to half create them and their impressions. Campbell did not long mull his question but answered it swiftly, explaining, "Tis distance lends enchantment to the view, / And robes the mountain in its azure hue." With its spacious skies, amber waves of grain, and the majesty of purple mountains above the fruited plain, "America the Beautiful" is similarly Romantic.

Romanticism comes easier to the young than to the old. Intellectual glaucoma clouds the vision of the young enabling them to fabricate views and imagine the sublime. For the old, views are short and clear, often unhappily so. In the words of the gospel song, the old have seen the light. Regrettably, the light does not always strip away darkness and sorrow. Instead it exposes the landscape of a failed state, its skies clouded by violence, spikes of wheat transformed into gun barrels, its plains eroded and poisoned by exploitation, and its fruits wormy with ethnic tribalism and cankered exceptionalism. "America the beautiful," as an expatriate put it, "has become America the ugly, and the dangerous." But for the Coleridgean oldster, sight need not reveal the grim. If person's view is short and particular, not distant or abstract, he may discover not so much likenesses as likeable things. These will make him feel part of and appreciate place after which the grating doings of others will stop sweeping like motes across the musing eye. For a moment he may disappear into looking.

  The eyes of my jogging partner David have so deteriorated that he can't discern perspective and a sidewalk crack could spill and break him. As a result, no longer do we lope the countryside. Instead we run laps on the track surrounding the soccer field. Actually, we creep. We have outgrown competition. Even if we were capable of speed, we wouldn't race. We agree with Arthur Helps who wrote, there are "more good words to be said against Competition than for it. No doubt, it is a great incentive to exertion; but there its function for good begins and ends. It is no friend to Love; and is first cousin, with no removes to Envy. Then it deranges and puts out of place the best motives for exertion." We keep Helps's opinion to ourselves. The youngsters who train on the lanes around us haven't aged into sensible maturity and would not understand his remarks. Moreover explaining motives is difficult and generally unsatisfactory. In December, a reporter asked what "propelled" me to spend so much of my life writing. I answered truthfully, "I don't know."

In any case on the track last week a jocular stranger addressed us, saying, "The only way to time you guys is with a calendar." For ninety minutes we circle the field, varying our route by sometimes shuffling clockwise, other times counterclockwise. To the unobservant the routine may seem confining and as unnatural and artificial as the polyurethane surface of the track and the rubbery turf of the field itself. Although limitation cages, it also focuses making a person aware of the immediate. For weeks this summer, sand wasps swarmed the jumping pits beside the track. They built nests underground by sweeping sand aside and digging holes for their larvae. The holes looked like dimples. The number of wasps zagging back and forth over the sand was uncountable. In two decades of running on the track, I'd never seen the wasps before. They were small, but their abdomens shook like flags, usually black and yellow but sometimes white and black. I overlooked the wasps because in past years I ran faster, my attention bound to time and distance. Not only had my pace deteriorated into timelessness, but I was no longer upright. Because I jogged slowly and leaned, I saw the wasps.

Before I retired, academic duties occupied most of my every day. Now happenstance determines the course of my hours, and one slight observation often leads to another. Moreover, if truth must out, what I once thought trifling now suggests likeness and, kindles affection for the world. One morning I noticed wild bergamot blooming on the gray hill rising from the edge of the track to a pallet of cardboard dormitories. A counterpane of thousands of flowers turned the slope lilac. Around every flowerhead bumblebees flurried and hovered, their wings beating up-tempo. On the stillest days the hill was alive. The bees shook the bergamot like a breeze, and the flowers wavered inhaling and exhaling. Later in the summer yellow patches of Jerusalem artichoke appeared amid the bergamot turning the slope sunny but somnolent, a transformation that coincided with the heat and humidity's wearing me down, limiting each day's jog to three miles.

The time that I once expended running more miles I now spent sitting on a folding chair in the driveway in front of my garage. The driveway was my porch. I drank tea and waved to passersby, most of whom were Indian and Chinese graduate students walking to and from their labs. Occasionally a neighbor stopped and chatted. We did not discuss front-page political controversies. We've learned they are ephemeral, and the storm of cliches that accompanies such talk muddies mood and drowns good sense. We usually began by bemoaning the virus but then concluded by agreeing that the way we lived hadn't changed much, "except," as a one woman put it, "I have more time for gardening, something I love to do." Because I sat quietly, life came to me. Deer ambled across the yard grazing on mushrooms, often varieties of russula and agaricus, the favorite among the latter, horse mushrooms. After a serving of mushroom, the deer rinsed their mouths with clumps of minty gill-over-the-ground. One day three hen turkeys and eleven chicks wandered into the woods behind the house. I hadn't seen turkeys in the yard before, and I assume they appeared because the virus purged cars from our street. Late in the summer squirrels began pruning twigs off trees, especially red oaks, sugar and Norway maples. Arborists aren't sure why squirrels clip twigs. I believe they do so to sharpen their teeth, or when I am in irritable mood, I decide they have learned from man and copying his anti-social behavior do it to be a nuisance.

To say that mushrooms came to me is silly. However, they materialized silently and mysteriously, suddenly appearing: russulas with starched stems and brick red caps sinking like navels, dingy gray lactarius, small apricot-colored chanterelles, and boletus, its spongy caps tilting atop blocky stems and looking worn and upholstered. Because I spent much time in the yard, I noticed plants so familiar that I had not seen them for years. Beneath the neglected bird feeder, a rough coil of day lilies bloomed. From the center of the flowers, hot yellow stars flared upward causing the orange petals to roll and crinkle. Ramp lost leaves and in the understory of woods slunk from sight becoming naked stalks supporting small umbels of white flowers. Some forty Indian pipes burst through the dark ground in a fountain tighter than a wrist of water before tumbling into sprays of spumy flowers. In the sunlight plants turned moments watery. Along the property line gooseneck loosestrife bloomed forming a white pool, its spikes of flowers arching and glistening.

I didn't spend all my days in the driveway, but when I left home, I walked so slowly I might as well have been sitting. On the campus Norway maples were lofts of samaras with four-inch wingspreads. Persian silk trees bloomed so profusely that they seemed covered by a light pink snow. Rays fell back and under the buttons of sneezeweed looking like scalloped skirts, yellow and buttery, whirling and melting. Robes and starry crowns don't suit me, and when the roll is called up yonder, I'll be elsewhere. Never have I ambled down to water to pray as the gospel song puts it. However, reverence arises out of sense experience, and looking has often assured me that a "better home" doesn't await in the sky but exists in the here-and-now living, observable world. In Mirror Lake a muskrat built a lodge, and turtles sunned on a log gleaming like black satin tuxedo buttons. A cormorant spread it wings like a Roman standard. Nearby a great blue heron stood motionless as a rail. Amid rocks in the shallows of the Fenton River, shafts of cardinal flower were racks of candied blossoms. On a bank above the river, royal blue flowers wrapped the spikes of vervain like bunting. An eastern amberwing dragonfly perched on a tussock sedge beside a pond, its wings more orange than amber, waving and mesmerizing.

    Because I had time for them, insects had time for me. Amid the pachysandra by the driveway lurked the pale nymph of a snowy tree cricket. Under a sheaf of bark lay an eyed click beetle. White lightener circled the black "eyes" atop the prothorax creating a bulbous intimidating effect. A grapevine beetle clung to the clematis beside the back door. The beetle was polished and ochre, a transformation from two larval years crawling amid stumps and tree roots. A dark lyric cicada provided the happiest insect surprise bumping into me as I sat in the driveway. The cicada was black except for a small green design on its upper back resembling a keyhole or, as one entomologist put it, "a soda pop pull tab." Dark lyric cicadas sing in the evening, their songs electric buzzes that wind up then down as people turn on house lights.

In my family roots dig deeper than those of sweetgum and white oak. Two weeks ago, Eliza sent me photos she copied from an album that belonged to Mother. The pictures were taken in Nashville and depicted our happy family thirty-three years ago. Francis was seven, Edward five, and Eliza three. The children were jubilant, and Vicki's smile was brighter than the sunrise. Within three years Mother and Father would be dead, but for the moment they were alive loving and being loved. "Why did those years vanish," I asked as I sat by myself in the driveway. "They were so luminous; why aren't they always blooming in memory?" The recollections evoked by the pictures gave the lie to my books—the pages of ordered, whitened, almost classical prose, the studious avoidance of the personal, especially the emotional. "Nuts," I muttered, "I wrote as much to obscure as I did to reveal and celebrate." Of course, Southerners formed by manners and propriety couldn't act otherwise. "I curbed, trimmed, and balanced. I didn't stray beyond margins," I thought, "because that was best for others, and probably best for me as well." Why, I have long wondered, do so many autobiographers depict relatives as Satanists? Does ego induce writers to appear self-created? Does it make them want to seem sui generis, individuals who overcame hardship and outgrew the parochial and who are now on the angelic side of everything? But then perhaps few people had parents as decent and responsible as mine.

Only the old understand the loneliness of old age, and indeed the weariness. Bookishness is usually an anodyne, but sometimes a page puts feelings into an assuaging context and for the aged reader serves as a crutch. As I sat holding the pictures, I recalled Frost's poem "Nothing Gold Can Stay." "Nature's first green is gold, / Her hardest hue to hold. / Her early leaf's a flower; / But only so an hour. / Then leaf subsides to leaf, / So Eden sank to grief, / So dawn goes down to day. / Nothing gold can stay." As students returned to the university, so the quiet street in front of the house became an abattoir. At five one morning I shoveled a ground hog off the road. The deaths of animals depress Vicki, and before she woke, I buried the groundhog in the woods behind the house. I thought the hole I dug cavernous. I was wrong. It wasn't deep enough to deter Reddy Fox, and the three days later I reburied the groundhog who had aged into being picante and as such into an alluring main course.

 The times I spend behind the wheel now strike me as times on the wheel. I prefer sitting to driving. When I sally from the yard, I usually roam wood and field, getting there by walking rather than riding. However, I've aged into wilt and canker, and necessity, or perhaps an inordinate hankering to avoid becoming the groundhog's slumber companion for a few seasons more, forces me to visit doctors. There I meet people suffering from sundry necroses and "who keep hospitals solvent," remarked a friend who for years abjured medicine and is now delectating in the balsamic pleasures of an earth bath. In a waiting room I recently talked to a woman suffering from diabetes, COPD, and diseases caused by pathogens so unfamiliar they seemed almost Romantic. Prey, so far as I could tell, to an assortment rusts and rots, a man waiting for a CAT-scan was so nervous he vomited. A woman described the terrible plight of her younger brother. He'd caught the coronavirus and after two tense weeks in a hospital returned home. "He was cured, but he wasn't, and I worry that he can never be cured," the woman told me. In the past two and a half months, he had gone to the emergency room twenty-four times, wracked by pains and shocks. Sometimes he couldn't move an arm or a leg. Other times he had palsy and his arms and legs shook spasmodically. His heart "felt like it was cracking." He couldn't smell or taste. He could not think, and his head "throbbed like someone was hitting it with a hammer."

The nature that youth observes is not the nature age sees. Coleridge was twenty-nine when he said that people felt soothed by likenesses they perceived between themselves and rural nature. Coleridge did not mention anthracnose, black knot, and lethal yellowing. Perhaps he didn't notice them. However, if he accompanied me to hospital waiting rooms, he could not ignore galls and blights. Instead of thinking differences between man and nature and between people themselves to be sources of ill will and hatred, he might have thought some differences between aged trees and the elderly were signs of health. How nice for an oldster not to receive the diagnosis of his withering contemporaries but that of a sapling: solid heartwood, cholesterol free sap, and a crown untouched by dementia.

The why's of life are usually inexplicable. People have many roots in addition to the one that digs through the years to buried family memory. One night last month I dreamed I was in Atlanta watching the construction of four major highways. The pavement on each was a different color: red, blue, green, and gray. The supervisor wore a yellow vest and an earring shaped like a cross on the lobe of his left ear. The next morning in my imagined class students handed in essays. In his essay a boy described my dream including details about the earring and the colors of the roads. I had not mentioned the dream to the class. What, I wondered, did the boy's essay imply about the relations of things. I did not reach a conclusion because the boy suffered from fourth-stage like-itis. When I inquired about the provenance of his paper, he stuttered into a volley of likes saying, "I'm like, like 'oh my god,' I'm like. Like don't you see I'm like?" I couldn't tolerate the absence of sensible speech, and I woke myself up without discovering how the boy learned about my visit to Atlanta. *Like* is just one of many fillers that infect contemporary speech, particularly the talk of college graduates. Not long ago my friend Josh said that among gridiron alumni from pigskin conferences, *hut* is a glottal commonplace "highlighting the conversation" of superannuated quarterbacks and centers, as well as wide receivers, kickers, college presidents, and cheerleaders. Mid-way through football autumn, Josh heard a former tackle say, "I'm hut, hut one, not two, oh my god, hut, hut, what ho, hut—what?" The man wasn't explaining, Josh elaborated, his long-standing scholarly interest in Proust.

Since childhood I've wandered distant lands, traveling in ships and trains, on foot, horseback, and camelback and, perhaps most frequently by books. The coronavirus didn't imprison me. Instead of visiting the faraway, I explored home journeying at night on box springs and a mattress. Although the souvenirs I collected won't be displayed at a tag sale, they were intriguing, albeit tainted by the rococo. In a dream recently I flew from Slovenia to India. Because I was asleep and dreaming, I didn't notice the Transylvanian Alps, Caspian Sea, or the Plateau of Iran. I awoke only as the plane landed in Hyderabad. What puzzled me was why since I was already asleep and dreaming did I dream that I was asleep and dreaming. Life, of course, is repetitious and cluttered with redundancies. Nevertheless, the double helping of sleep topped with two servings of dreams seemed odd, if not too much for a temperate person's midnight snack.

Such matters make good driveway ponderings. They accompany tea and banana bread well. In the daylight they don't cause indigestion. Neither do they disturb soothing Coleridgean moods when a lounger notices a meadow katydid clinging to the last daylily of summer or an obscure underwing moth gray and camouflaged clinging to the rough plates of a shagbark hickory. They don't undermine the surprise of seeing clusters of hen of the woods mushrooms suddenly appear near stumps and atop the roots of dead trees and then rapidly swell into heavy flaky boutonnieres. The cluster nearest my chair was nine inches high and twenty-two wide. In the quiet one hears the symphonies of summer: the stuttering of great horned owls, kingfishers jangling, tambourines of newly fledged Carolina wrens, the metallic scraping cries of red-tailed hawks, and always the doleful songs of mourning doves. For many years I thought they were called morning doves, their songs suited to oldsters waking in the gray before dawn and struggling to cajole their arthritic bodies to shift from bedside perches to floor boards.

If a person listens carefully, he can hear silent sounds; the rhapsody of clouds, the staccato zithering of white corporal dragonflies and bows of wind siding across the finely wrought stamens of blue curls. For the person attuned to nature, more often than not raucous sounds become music and tranquilize. At twilight little brown bats cut and twist above the house, their flights popping like the sound of the bodhran. At night concerts of crickets, katydids, and cicadas sweep through the trees and over the yard wrapping me like an eiderdown and lulling me to sleep. Such moods are not long-lived. Inexorably Time fractures them. Cicadas vanish from the night. I return my folding chair to the garage, and grimmer, more realistic thoughts come to mind. Not even teas of yarrow and boneset, gargles of purple loosestrife and Asiatic dayflower, and lozenges of wild hydrangea and Queen Anne's lace can prevent the intrusion of medical matters.

Retired teachers, my friend Josh said last year, "are corpses in waiting neglected by puddle-jumping administrators who don't know any of us." Beyond our front doors, the only people aware of us are doctors, Josh continued. "Teachers clean out their offices and move from the classroom to the operating room. From parsing sentences to have their parts parsed." Although outspoken, Josh is often perceptive. Recently, I've stopped napping in the driveway and begun dozing in waiting rooms. Two weeks ago, a doctor gave me a hormone shot, "a testosterone suppressor." The classically educated call it "the Teiresias injection" and predict that after my hair grows long, I will have it styled. "You can start a new career and become Connecticut's favorite weather doxy." Others less inclined to Greek ways call the shot "the Castrator." Among its side effects are slack muscles, a fetching bosom, a mid-drift similar to that of a belly dancer, and hot flashes. "I may be a little blowsy," I told Vicki. "You've always been blowsy," she replied. "Even if I occasionally I say naughties like 'oh, sugar?'" I said. "Especially then," Vicki said ending the conversation with a spicy expletive which respectable linguistic cooks use only in pinches.

I should add that an infusion of valerian to keep my spirits up is unnecessary. I have no plans to unearth the lightning rod that's stored in the garage and going outside during a thunderstorm raise the rod over my head. Last Thursday a television in the reception room of an oncology clinic was tuned to a game show. When I walked into the room, the show broke for "messages from our sponsors." Prominent among them was a company peddling funeral and burial insurance. In the advertisement appeared a gaggle of smiling widows and widowers, ecstatic to escape sickrooms and pocketing bundles of unexpected cash eager to flock South for sun and surf and friends anew. "Damn," I said and laughed. No one else in the room smiled. They probably needed thumping good doses of juice squeezed out of pink lady's slippers, not a flower I saw many of this year. How different this spring was from that of last year—no gypsy moth caterpillars and no blossoms on mountain laurel but rain forests of monkey flowers, their petals a happier blue than that of any imagined heaven.

Radioactive

People who live long realize that ailments are natural parts of a full life. Being diagnosed with cancer upsets but doesn't surprise them. Moreover, sometimes a disease broadens life rather than reduces it. Of course, many people react to misfortune by creating fictions to ease living as well as dying, religion with its promise of unending and compensatory bliss being prominent. At their most utilitarian, grandchildren animate the imagination and shift the attention of the elderly from their own lives. Grandchildren cause people to repress the splenetic lessons taught in the schoolhouse of years and to envision fantasies of happiness and hope, of decency recognized and virtue rewarded, to fabricate fairy tales of futures shiny with glass slippers and green with climbable beanstalks.

Sometimes I wonder if writing has insulated me from being unduly bothered by my pipes' rusting into aches and pains. "No," Vicki said, "little things distract you more than they do most people. Remember last spring when we were sitting on a bench outside the Benton Museum. The Yoshimo cherries were pompoms of pink and white blossoms. I was giving the dogs a treat, and you were looking at a scrap of paper you found on the ground." I am a peripatetic yardman and pick up trash throughout the day. Sometimes I unravel papers and read what is written on them. The sheet to which Vicki referred was a questionnaire, part of an application filled by students eager to join an all-male a cappella group. Questions asked the applicant his name, telephone number, voice part, musical experience, whether he could beatbox and read music, jobs he'd held on campus, and the hours he was free to rehearse, for this last choosing from three selected times.

Fred my applicant was available at all the listed times, was a finance major, a tenor One, and once sang the national anthem before a baseball game at Yankee Stadium. The only playful section on the questionnaire asked the applicant his "Best Pickup Line." Fred did well for a sophomore finance major. "Hey, sorry to bother you," he said to a classmate as they left a lecture hall. "My hands are full of books. Do you mind reaching into my jacket pocket and getting my phone?" After the girl fetched his phone, Fred said, "Thank you," then requested, "Now would you please put your number in it?" "Not so good," Vicki said after I read Fred's lines to her. "Unseasoned namby-pamby stuff; 'hi,' or 'hey, cutie pie' would be to the point and their jabber wouldn't plug the door to the classroom. Even better would be the old standby, 'what's up, Sugar Ti.'" "Stop," I said before the Vicki tacked the final two consonants onto "ti." "If you knew Vicki like I know Vicki," I told Josh later, "you'd have stopped her, too."

Writing also blurs my focus and shifts thoughts from myself onto other things. Rarely does the daily news pass without an account of what purports to be a bolstering fiction. Outside nursing homes and senior centers signs proclaiming "Old Lives Matter" have suddenly metastasized. Billboards have appeared in New Jersey, Delaware, Pennsylvania, and Oklahoma among a landscape of other states. Such signs are exclusionary and tribal and repel me. What matters to me are trees and flowers, birds, clear streams, and spacious skies pure and white with cumulous clouds, that is, the environment, life forms not dear to the corporatizing, acquisitive class. Would that I believed that such things mattered to vast numbers of influential people. If they did, the earth and those of us who inhabit this moment would be healthier. But I am not a believer. "Nobody knows anything of the world around them. By which I mean the physical, actual world," my son Edward lamented last year. "Find a person who can discriminate between species of oak. Or knows the first thing about soil composition. Or knows the moon phases. Or has knowledge of any traditional craft. We're divorced from it all, almost all of us—consumers in a world economy that mass produces things in who-knows-where. And we exist only online where we argue about identity."

In *Borges and Me* Jay Parini described travelling the highlands of Scotland fifty years ago with Jorge Luis Borges the great Argentinean writer. Before setting out Parini was hesitant, and Borges urged him on, saying, "We must take the plunge. What we discover, as within any labyrinth, will always be ourselves." In a sense the whole of life is a labyrinth in which a person discovers much more than himself. At the moment I am undergoing—exploring is probably more accurate—a nine-week regimen of radiation at the Helen and Harry Gray Cancer Center in Hartford. I have completed 41 of 43 sessions and am over 95 percent of the way through. "The prostate guys," Michael a technician told me, "schedule more treatments than the other doctors." On week nights, I go to bed at 8:30. My rest is fitful and intermittent. The radiation causes frequent visits to the lavatory, and no period of sleep lasts longer than 50 minutes. Moreover, an injection that represses testosterone causes night sweats. Throughout the night I wake and dripping perspiration kick off the blankets. Soon afterward I am damp and cold and pulling the blankets up to my neck to snuggle against Vicki treating her as a space heater. On the positive side of things, the sweats warm me, and on cold days when I work outside, I don't have to wrap myself in sweaters. Moreover, the sweats prevent my turning into a block of ice when I jog.

Pliny, The Younger, said the lives of old men should be regular and methodical, adding that with youth some confusion and irregularity were not unbecoming. My ways could serve as a philosophical and pharmaceutical example of the course of life admired by Pliny. Five days a week I get out of bed at 4:30. I take care of ablutions, eat a small breakfast composed of fruit and granola, and put the dogs out in the back yard. I am at their beck and yap, and after twelve minutes I bring them back and lock them in the kitchen. I leave the house at ten minutes before six and drive to Hartford. A little after seven, I'm radiated. By 8:20, I am home sitting at the kitchen table eating a second small breakfast. Because the doctor directed that my bladder should be full when I undergo the radiation, I drink two cups of Yorkshire tea during the first breakfast. To follow the prescription, I carry two eight-ounce bottles of water in the car and drink while driving. On the floor of the passenger side of the front seat I carry a portable necessary house consisting of a bucket, towel, and plastic hospital urinal. So far, the lavatory has served only to allay worry.

On the two occasions when a pipe fitting loosened, I stopped beside the road, something I've done countless times. I don't wave at passersby, but pulling onto a shoulder to answer a call of nature has never bothered me. In "Stopping by Woods on a Snowy Evening," Frost's narrator recalled that his "little horse" thought it odd "to stop without a farm house near." The narrator said that he paused to watch snowflakes fall through the trees. He noted that the owner of the woodlot lived some distance away in a village and wouldn't notice his presence. Wondering why his rider stopped, the horse became impatient and shook his harness bells "to ask if there is some mistake." The horse was mystified and the narrator less than forthcoming, but every man of a certain age knows why the traveler broke his journey. Necessity summoned him, a less poetic imperative but one more pressing than stopping to appreciate "the sweep of easy wind and downy flake." "Leaving one's car on a cold night to urinate against a tree? What sort of poem would that make?" Josh asked then answered his own question. "A short one—a sonnet. Content determines form."

I am the Chingachgook of the road. My way is clearly marked, and I know it well. After leaving the house I creep across the university campus passing through one traffic light and seven stop signs. At the edge of the campus I turn west on Route 44 and drive for ten miles going through eight stoplights. I then leave 44 and enter Interstate 384 at Bolton. Six miles farther on, the road joins 84, and I follow it for three and a half miles into Hartford. Before arriving at the Center, I pass through eleven more traffic lights, raising the total to twenty. The drives to and from Hartford take forty minutes each way. A round trip consists of fifty-three miles, thus at the conclusion of my appointments I will have driven 2279 miles. Driving to is more difficult than driving from Hartford because the sun has not risen, and members of the morons' one-hundred-mile-an-hour automobile lodge delight in perfecting their lane-changing skills in the dark. Members are easily recognizable. Initiates drive low red, black, and white cars, often with megaphone mufflers enabling them to be heard before they are seen. The significance of the colors is a quasi-masonic secret, but it is obvious that the drivers don't give a gasket about other people's lives. The fraternity ought to be banned from the road. Once safely ensconced in driveways, responsible, mild-mannered motorists slam the doors to their cars and stomping like Rumpelstiltskin, shout, labeling members of the brotherhood "jackasses" and "God damn idiots," these being the two politest appellations.

On each trip I experience at least two white-knuckle incidents. The most terrifying section of the drive is the juncture of 84 and 384 where cars pour together erratically like water streaming out of pipes blocked by air. Of course, driving sparks endless concerns. I worry that the car, Vicki's and my only car, will break down before I finish the treatments. One morning a yellow light appeared on the dashboard warning that the air in my tires was low. On returning from Hartford, I paused at home long enough to brew a jolting cup of tea. I then set out for Holmgren Subaru, fifteen miles east in North Franklin. The tires were all right, the pressure reflecting, a mechanic told me, the recent dip in temperature. The primary side effects of my driving are weariness and dislike of the road, indeed for all things vehicular. Escape from spending hours on asphalt is, of course, impossible. One Wednesday after returning from Hartford, I chauffeured Vicki to an eye examination in West Hartford.

Her appointment was at two o'clock. We left slightly before one and got to the doctor's office on time. Because of the virus, only patients were admitted to the office. I sat outside the building on a bench and read until Vicki came out at 4:45. On days when Vicki walks the dogs on campus, she stops at the student center for coffee. Every day the same woman makes the coffee, and she and Vicki chat. Vicki wanted to buy her a present, so after leaving the eye doctor's office, I drove to Evergreen Mall in Buckland. There Vicki purchased a half pound of dark chocolate at Munson's for the woman. The roads were impacted. From the candy store, I drove to Panera where we ate dinner. We left the restaurant at seven o'clock. "At least the roads won't be crowded," Vicki said. Vicki was wrong. A cloudburst of Metamucil could not have cleared the interstate. We reached home at 7:45, and I went to bed to ready myself for getting up the next morning at 4:30.

 I generally arrive at the Center ten minutes before the door opens at 6:45. The parking lot is empty and after I slot the car into my habitual place, I chat with staff waiting to enter the building. Masks make recognizing faces difficult. However, I am able to identify individuals by their strides and the shape of their shoulders. At the entrance we talk about the usual things: the weather, family ailments, retirement, and the corruption and betrayals of politicians. One morning Carol brought a shopping bag of cat food. For years a feral cat has hung around the building. "He's skinny," Carol said, "and I'm going to fatten him up." Because her husband has early-onset dementia and is homebound, Carol holds two jobs to support her family. Nonetheless, she also cares for human strays. "She gives them money for food, never less than ten dollars," another nurse told me. "She realizes that most of the time the money goes for drugs or drink, but she is the good Samaritan. She helps homeless people find housing and directs them to soup kitchens." The staff are the human face of the Center, and the day before Carol left for a short vacation, I handed her twenty dollars for cat food. I gave Carol the money more for me than the cat—to create a momentary liking for myself. Along the parking lot banners hang from light poles. Aside from the absence of dog muzzles and the different words stamped on them, the banners are the same as those at the university, that is, corporatized branding and advertising. While the Heart and Vascular Institute offers Cardiac Care, Comprehensive Neuroscience Care can be found at the Ayer Neuroscience Institute. At the Cancer Institute people will discover "More Options, More Hope." The neighborhood across from the Center is scuffed. The one time I wandered beyond the parking lot, I returned after noticing a placard taped to an apartment building. "Smile. You're on Camera," it stated in hopes of discouraging loiterers. I interpreted the placard as advising me to "Stop," make a U-turn, and go back to the Center.

Inside the building Helen greets me by name and takes my temperature. Never has my temperature climbed above 95.4 degrees. Generally, it is 95.1. "You are a cold one," she says. For seven weeks Helen wielded an ear thermometer that had a disposable metal tip. Helen only tests patients. Nurses take their temperatures with cell phones at home and send the results to the Center. During a four-day period, Helen and the other people at the front desk used 1044 tips. Toward the end of my treatments, a Tauri temperature machine appeared. The Tauri is five feet tall. Attached to the top is a tilted screen. A patient approaches the screen until his face becomes visible, in my case four feet away. Then the machine measures his temperature. "The machine cost more than I am worth on the hoof or off," I said to Helen. "More than both of us," she replied. Early in October a stack of pink T-shirts appeared on a desk in the lobby. "For staff members to wear during Breast Cancer Awareness Month," a nurse explained then asked, "maybe next October ought to be Prostate Cancer Month. What color should the shirt be?" Never had I pondered medical sartorials. But I suppose as a guy with prostate cancer, my "opinion mattered." "Magenta," I said boldly, and unaccountably. "A good choice," the nurse said, "people will notice the color." "Exactly," I replied.

The main lobby is a large high-ceilinged shoe box shaped room. From it corridors lead into three departments: Radiation Oncology, Medical Oncology, and the Infusion Center. The lobby is dull but comfortable with tables, couches, chairs, and surprisingly a grand piano, played, I assume, during fund-raising events. Standing before the door leading into the Infusion Center is the single interesting decoration in the room: the replica of a cow. The cow is waist-high and almost full-sized. She has dreamy googly eyes and long weepy eyelashes. She looks like a Brown Swiss but could have an illegitimate touch of Jersey in her DNA. She wears an old-fashioned nurse's uniform: a white blouse and a white skirt. Her feet are not hooves but soft white shoes. Perched on her head between her horns is a nurse's cap with a red cross on the front. Over her mouth and nose, a herdsman has taped a white coronavirus mask. Dangling from her neck are a stethoscope and a rectangular sign the size of a license plate with "Peace" printed on it in green letters. I asked several people who worked in the Center the name of the cow. None knew. Not aware that cows grew horns and never having noticed the nurse's costume, one doctor speculated that the cow was a bull. Eventually I named the cow Ida after my grandmother Ida Ratcliffe. At Cabin Hill, she and Grandpa Ratcliffe owned a milking herd of Jerseys and Guernseys. To insure that Ida was not forgotten, I told people the name and several mornings gave them pop quizzes.

Appointments at the Center broadened my thoughts, and the hard divider between past and future softened. Grandpa had several interests and businesses in addition to the dairy. He was also a florist and grew and experimented with plants. Boxwoods were his favorite shrub, and he planted thousands at Cabin Hill. They were also my favorites, and when I was young, the leaves were my chewing tobacco. At funerals two hundred years ago, mourners who accompanied a corpse to cemetery sometimes carried sprigs of box. They tossed them atop the coffin after it was lowered into the grave. In the Victorian Age when a death occurred in a house, people occasionally hung boxwood wreathes on their front doors. During the course of my treatments, White Flower Farm's holiday catalogue arrived. It advertised baskets and cachepots of amaryllis, vases and potting trays of paperwhites, garlands of edible ornaments to attract birds, and pages of Christmas wreathes. Among these last was the "Festive Boxwood Wreath" adorned with red Canella berries, not the mourning wreath's black bows. To me a cemetery in which box are not planted beside tombstones is lifeless, too sterile to resuscitate happy memories. Only when graves are green with box can conversation with the dead flourish. The regimen in Hartford quickened, not lessened, living, and this Christmas Vicki and I will hang a boxwood wreath on the front door, not a dolorous sign of ending but one of continuance, green and joyous with hope, good will, high spirits, and smiling memories.

Among the better ways to establish one's name is to name other things. Ida awakened the desire to make a mark, a hankering that the radiation had practically eradicated. I have since named Carol's cat "Don't Know." Because the number of gay bachelors roaming local alleys is legion, I rejected the name Thomas. To select an appropriate name, I instituted a survey. In it I followed Pew's methodological model and collected data meticulously. I interviewed five nurses and asked them the name of the cat. To guard against their immediately grasping the intention of the survey, I buried this essential query under a plethora of "remarkage," interrogatives such as, "Good morning, how are you today?" "Boy, isn't it chilly?" and "Did you get that coffee in the luncheonette across the street?" In response to the matter of nomenclature, three of my five subjects said, "Don't Know." While one of the remaining nurses thought the name to be "What," the other believed it was "Huh." Clearly, these last two were idiosyncratic outliners. Sixty per cent agreement is a workable majority, and I have pressed "Don't Know" into the consciousness of the people I meet each morning at the Center, not just cat fanciers but also psittaculturists, aquarists, and dog aficionadas.

The hall leading from the main lobby to the small waiting area in Radiation Oncology is broad, high-ceilinged, and light burlap in color bordered by blue and buttery gray doors and counter tops. "A bit like drops for dry eyes, bland and watery, not bright and piercing," a fellow patient said, "preaching, if walls can preach, endurance and calm." On the walls hang color photographs taken by Jack McConnell. Mounted on white in everyday black frames, most of the pictures are eighteen inches tall and two feet wide. Well-lit and scrubbed, they are sentimental and smack of neuropathic medicine and the benevolent, painless healing of natural beauty or, in literary terms, pharmacological Romanticism. If a person studies them, so the prescription runs, he might lose himself amid the beauty and for a moment forget his troubles. An Edenic New England blooms in the pictures: a field of ox-eyed daisies, shrubs of white roses, a trellis shaggy with red roses, a Japanese cherry, an expanse of yellow tulips, purple lilacs, and an apple orchard, all its branches pink with flowers. A stream tumbles over soft granite rocks into a royal blue pool. Barns and backhouses are dark red, and a sugar maple drifts into fall, its leaves sails of light yellow. Fields stretch mown and lyrical to the skirts of soft hills. Stone walls slump like the shoulders of old men. No wall has collapsed into a liver-spotted heap. Time and rain have worn the edges off the stones, and they clump together in quiet round comfort, none needing rotator cuffs ground away. "No garbage dumps flapping with seagulls, Styrofoam buckets of half-eaten fried chicken, floss picks, hypodermic needles, or ruined men and woman sleeping in cardboard boxes," I said, adding, "not the vision of Hieronymus Bosch." "No," said Bob a "Jack of All Machines" whom I lassoed and corralled every morning. "Bosch painted truths recognized by people who have outlived youthful enthusiasm for Thoreau." Bosch's paintings wouldn't be therapeutic. They'd depress the spirits of patients hoping that their cancers can be cured. The stone walls in the photographs do not make a prison. Instead they spring Lovelace's iron gates and afford glimpses of a New England pulsing with so much beauty that it awakens dreams of imagined pasts and improbable futures. Most mornings Bob and I chat. Our conversation rambles as it does with men of a certain age who are at ease with each other. We discuss a miscellany of things: education and the University of Connecticut, repairing roofs, Caribbean islands, puzzles and board games, in this last comparing the play of people with literary bents to those inclined toward mathematics, and then gathering seeds from ancient trees and planting them. Some of the biggest and oldest trees in Hartford, Bob said, "are on the grounds of the Institute for Living. The oaks and lindens are especially beautiful, and walking beneath them is inspirational."

Conversation in the prostate klatch is often more cultural than that I remembered in the English Department. Certainly, there is much shop talk as men compare PSA's and the number of radiation treatments. The treatments of women generally do not last as many days as those of men, and as a result women are associate rather than full members of the klatch. Once two discussed creatures that frightened them: snakes, spiders, and moths. "The lasting effects of herd education and aping girlish hysteria," one woman opined. Another morning I wore a short-sleeved shirt decorated with hummingbirds. Seven dashed across my chest, and ten on my back hovered over columbine and blue delphiniums. "Look at this. We are cousins," a woman said, pointing to a tattoo on the outside of her right ankle. A hummingbird hung over a hybrid flower, part day lily and part trumpet vine. Ink in the bird's feathers had lost definition and run into scrubby blue. "She isn't much bird now, but once upon a time," the woman said, "she was a high flyer, colorful and lively and loved to kick up her wings."

Like behavior thoughts are not solitary. The hummingbird did not spritz out of mind into flight, and as the woman talked, I recalled other tattoos. Not long after her mother's burial my friend Adelaide took an armful of flowers to her grave in Mt. Olivet cemetery in Nashville. While she was stooped over placing the flowers in a garden vase beside the headstone, a tiger swallowtail butterfly lit on Adelaide's back just above the left shoulder blade. "That was Mother's spirit," she told me. "She loved butterflies and planted butterfly bushes around her yard." To remain close to her mother's "beautiful spirit," Adelaide had a swallowtail tattooed on her back. "Whenever I am on the verge of doing or saying something regrettable, Mother flutters and urges restraint."

Climate change, habitat destruction, and pesticides have reduced the numbers of insects swatting them from daily life. Where they have thrived, however, is on the fleshly human landscape. Honeybees may no longer pollinate flowers but they swarm across all parts of people's anatomies. No matter where a person roams, be it the sandiest desert or the wide abandoned sea, he will see dragonflies sunning on arms, legs, chests, or hanging from earrings and dangling from necklaces. The most thoughtful tattoo I've seen appeared on the calf of a Phi Beta Kappa. A lightning bug sat at a desk in a wooden Hitchcock chair. The last segment of the bug's abdomen was luminous and stuck through the slats on the back of the chair. Held upright on the desk by the insect's first four legs was a book. Printed on the cover in thick red letters was "DESCARTES."

Of the many tattoos in the Anatomy Hall of Fame, the one I wish I had seen off the page was that of a Lieutenant Colonel who served in the Royal Artillery in World War I. After the war he settled in the wilds of Northern Rhodesia, now Zambia. There he built a small manor house and lived according to whim. He wore a monocle and on occasions when he entertained visitors dressed his house servants in trousers and tunics reminiscent of military uniforms. Generally, he wore a pith helmet, but sometimes he wore a battle bowler, that is, a steel Brodie helmet which when placed upside down on its crown looked like a salad bowl. He particularly enjoyed wearing the helmet on rainy days during which he stood on the front stoop of his house and listened to the drops pattering atop his head, "playing nocturnes." His tattoo was not so elevated, however. On his backside and trundling down his spine and disappearing into his gluteal cleft was a platoon of tumblebugs. Supposedly he got the tattoo after surviving Passchendaele in 1917, explaining his motivation by paraphrasing the King James Bible, saying, "Unto dust we shall all return."

Doings in the klatch are easy and pleasant. Rodney and I talked about horses. A farrier, he'd shod many Morgan horses owned by the university. He lived in a gingerbread Victorian dollhouse house in the old Methodist camp ground above Willimantic. He arrived at the Center shortly after me. By the end of my treatments, I recognized his truck by the pitch of its headlights even though he was three or so cars behind me on Wyllys Street. One morning a man's cellphone cackled like rooster. It was a wake-up call but because the man did not speak English, I did not learn what motivated the crowing. On another occasion, a Monday, Wednesday, and Friday visitor said, "the best thing about flossing before going to bed is that it enables a person to eat dinner twice." Henry told a light-hearted story about Hans Christian Andersen. In discussing arrangements for his death, Andersen requested that a small hole be drilled into his coffin. He explained that he wanted to peek out, enjoy the ceremony, and see who of his good friends followed him to the grave and who did not.

"Of the very great of this earth" who "certainly are very few, all detail is interesting," William Bogart stated at the beginning of *Who Goes There? or, Men and Events*, a collection of anecdotal descriptions of prominent men like Alexander Hamilton and Henry Clay. Scribblers are their own ardent apologists. I've never met anyone great. Thomas Carlyle argued that the history of the world was "but the biography of great men." From my perspective greatness seems tainted by platitude and often smudged by depravity. I live in a modest house beside a university campus, not in the expansive historical world. To me the remarks made by and the details of the lives of people who inhabit the everyday and who do not aspire to eminence seem true and revealing, and in a personal way, important. Of course, what else could a familiar essayist say? The mundane world is his theater, and for me that is better than good enough.

Before he completed his treatments, Frank and I chatted every morning. Since we met at the klatch and talked to get to know each other, the subjects were diverse yet personal: the happenstance nature of success, health insurance and the bills for our radiation, rowing, and summer camps in Maine. In the early 1960's I spent five summers as a counselor at Camp

Timanous in Raymond, Maine. Later my sons Francis and Edward spent sixteen summers there as campers and in Edward's case some of the summers as a counselor, When I learned that Frank's stepdaughters and my Eliza attended the sister camp of Timanous, Wohelo on Sebago Lake, I broke into song, singing, "O Wohelo. O Wohelo, Camp Timanous welcomes you to her domain." At "for you are Hiatini's camp, the best girls' camp in Maine," Frank joined me and we stood and pranced about the room. "Two eighty-year old's swinging and swaying," another patient said. "A sight for sore bodies." One morning during my first week of appointments, I staggered out of the radiation room clutching my lower back. "There is a short in the machine," I gasped. "It burns like the mischief, but it isn't serious enough to delay your treatment—if you can stand pain." "Oh, God!" a man exclaimed and bounded out of his chair, repeating, "Oh, my God!"

    The old saw "as a person lives, he learns," is nonsense. Young fools become old fools. I did not learn, but after that morning, I became less demonstrative. In fact, after returning home one day, I took my blood pressure. It was a somnolent 117 over 61. A television hangs on a wall in the waiting room. Generally, it's tuned to a shopping channel. Often the items advertised both astonished and bored me. For six payments of $49.95 each, I learned I could purchase the Shark IQ Robot vacuum cleaner. The vacuum cleaner was cordless and round and black. When still, it looked like an oversized hockey puck. When prowling for dirt, it scooted through rooms, its maw open and resembling the masticating part of a sting ray, eyes and tail lopped off, snout rounded, and gills clipped and trimmed. I'd never seen such a vacuum cleaner.

Suppose a man set his new purchase to work and forgetting about it took a nap on a rug in the living room. "What," I asked Frank, "what would happen when the vacuum cleaner finished its chores, returned to living room, and saw the man sleeping on the floor? Was it an omnivore that would race over and gnaw into him, sweeping hips and thighs, bladder, colon, and probably prostate, down its gullet?"

Printed on my file was a miscellany of information: my medical history detailing medications both those I took and those I once took, all the times I'd been sliced and diced starting with a tonsillectomy when I was four or thereabouts, and then other things such as height, weight, marital status, bugbears religious and political, and my age and birthday. I was born on September 30, and that morning when I appeared for my appointment, three technicians came into the waiting room and wished me "Happy Birthday." Would that someone wrapped a red ribbon around my bare mid-drift and that the morning's radiation had been iced, preferably with chocolate or if that was unavailable coconut. That, of course, was asking too much of celebrants both in Hartford and at home where Vicki radiated, rather microwaved, a slab of banana bread she discovered lost behind a tub of cottage cheese on the lower shelf of the kitchen icebox.

But how thoughtful the technicians were. They were part of a select group of well-wishers, including an old girlfriend from the Age of Shyness and Innocence, Billy born on the same day in the same year but in a different hospital in Nashville, Holland America Cruise Lines, the host of a morning radio show broadcast from Willimantic, Grove Atlantic Press, David bearing two thirty-six-ounce tubs of Virginia Diner Peanuts, and Francis, Edward, and my first cousin Sherry, all of whom telephoned. Raymond came to the house wearing a thick mask and gave me bottle of princely Pinot Noir. I will drink it in December after the radiation has cooled and I need a medicinal to warm my giblets. A week before my birthday Eliza flew in from California bringing my present, a pot of cactuses. After initially causing a small flap at airport security, the cactuses intrigued the personnel who gathered about wanting to know the names of the cactuses. Among the six plants in the pot were Gold Nugget, a hybrid sempervivum which looks like a boutonniere worn by political candidates and Cobweb Leek, another sempervivum consisting of a pile of small boutonnieres, these presented to ambitious cub scouts who have earned enough merit badges to achieve bobcat and puma status, the largest boutonnieres saved for lions who stuff flyers into mailboxes on their streets. Vicki thinks the plants a nuisance and says they are my babies. Every sunny morning, I put the pot outside atop the generator. My haworthia looks like a religious icon. Its leaves taper and rise resembling fingers on palms pressed beseechingly together in prayer. A little prayer or awareness would be handy if it reminded me to avoid the sinfully sharp spines of the pincushion cactus. Rarely does a day pass without an "ouch" accompanying my lifting the pot.

In the console behind the radiation theater at the hospital are nine screens making the area look like the control room of a spaceship. During each visit, the radiation itself lasts less than eight minutes. While I lie on a flat bed, a machine passes over my mid-section three times. Generally I fall asleep, but music plays nonstop. "Some people are very nervous, and the music helps them relax by diverting attention away from the treatments," a technician told me. "I'm not sure that the finality of 'this will be the last dance' and of 'another one bites the dust' reassures all patients," I said, adding that perhaps the sort of love common in "Ditty Wah Ditty" would not appeal to Bible Christians or Koranic Moslems. Moreover, I opined "the stuttering 'ba-ba-ba" beginning of "Barbara Ann" was liable to promote the heebie-jeebies and cause patients to twitch uncontrollably. I also listen to music on the car radio while driving to and from Hartford. Rarely do I listen long. Most of the music is cacophonous and features yellyhooing, this last a melodious archaic word for shouting. Only occasionally do I hear a genial familiar piece, for example, "Chattanooga Choo Choo" in which "nothing could be finer than to have ham 'n' eggs in Carolina." Almost never does an unfamiliar song appeal to me, the exception being "Birmingham Bertha" who pursued her faithless lover Southern Sam to Chicago. When she caught him, she promised, "like the police I will never release that man." Sam was a slippery travelling man, and I suspect that before Bertha could arrest his inclinations and lock him in love-cuffs, he was riding the Seminole Limited back to Birmingham. In any case a week later, I heard Big Maybelle imploring women to "Please stay away from my Sam."

    The journey to Hartford and back is long in anxiety but short in time. Once I got home at 7:54. Nevertheless, the trip saps my energy. It pushes the rest of the morning into the afternoon and sometimes the afternoon into evening. Despite this, my normal activities have continued, albeit at a slower pace. One Saturday I cut the lawn using my old pushmi-pullyu mower. Its namesake, Doctor Doolittle's wondrous creature had the body of a horse. Protruding from each end was a head. While one end of my mower grazed on grass in my yard, the other talked to me. It urged me to appreciate autumn. "Blowing and raking leaves will exhaust you, but the colors will be more beautiful than any woven into Isfahan's magical carpets. This could be your final fall. Don't miss the beauty. Heaven can't compare to it."

The weeks of radiation are not fall's only regimen. My yard is a forest of maples, hickories, and oaks. Every October I blow leaves into loose mounds. Afterward I sweep them into tighter, more manageable piles which I rake onto a tarpaulin. Then I drag the tarpaulin behind the house and dump the leaves in the woods. Clearing leaves off the yard takes three days. When the blower, or I, run low on gas, I take a Coca-Cola break. I don't drink from cans, and I pour the soda into a glass brimming with a glacier of ice. Because leaves fall at intervals, I clear the yard four times, thus spending twelve days blowing, raking, and toting. Some years, I spend an additional two days neatening, especially when neighbors delay raking until Christmas and their leaves migrate across the road. This year I mulled putting the chore off until after my oncology appointments ended. Last week, however, I tested the blower. Contrary to expectation, it broke hibernation and started immediately. In the past the blower dallied until pulling the starter cord irritated it causing fits of smokey coughing. One year I pulled the cord forty-two times, provoking exclamations which I hope no neighbor overheard. Because the blower started so easily this year, I immediately started moving leaves. Although I'll occasionally take weekdays off, I should finish the yard a fortnight after the end of my radiation. By happenstance, four days ago an old friend wrote to ask about my health. In his email he described an accident involving a leaf blower. "Last week," he wrote, "a friend of ours came home to find that her husband had managed to kill himself by falling off his roof with a leaf blower strapped to his back. We, his wife, and many others had warned him not to climb up there as he was in his 70s and in poor shape. On the day of his death, he waited until his wife went on an errand then strapped on his leaf blower and climbed away. I can only conclude that he was proving the adage that men generally die before their wives because they want to." "Good Lord," Vicki exclaimed. "You must be sensible. Don't strap on that machine unless I am here to supervise." "Certainly not," I answered. I'm reliable but not slavishly truthful. Because I'm not in perfect health, I'll stay earthbound. However, I am almost across the bridge leading from the Careless Seventies to the Cautious Eighties, and yesterday when Vicki went to Prince Chopper, I hustled into the garage and started the blower. Next, I hoisted it atop a garbage barrel, slipped my arms through the harness straps, and staggering into the yard began blowing. Insofar as wanting to die before Vicki, I cannot imagine living without her. Mother died three years before Father. Afterward when he mentioned her death, Father shook his head and said to me, "Sammy, it wasn't supposed to be this way. It wasn't supposed to be this way."

 Mine is a big world of little things. Even during medically-reduced and altered days, breaking habit is difficult. One afternoon I accompanied Vicki to Price Chopper and bought a lottery ticket. I follow routine and purchase a one-dollar ticket once every two months. Almost immediately I regret buying tickets. I do not throw them away, however. I place them on a counter in the kitchen and slide them under a bottle of Lea & Perrin's Worcestershire Sauce to lock them in place. Afterward I turn to Vicki and say, "God, I hope our number isn't drawn. Winning would ruin our lives. We'd become grasping and suspect the motives of friends and well-wishers. Even worse, we'd soon be resentful, angry that we won when we were too old to enjoy the money." The result of the drawing was salubrious. Not one of the six numbers on our ticket was drawn. In fact, when added our numbers amounted to 104, only 61% of the winning ticket's total of 171. Since childhood, numbers have intrigued me. While some children played word games, I toyed with figures. Nevertheless, I suspect that the radiation and the concomitant keeping track of my treatments, counting down from the low 40s through the 30s and the 20s, and now into the single digits has increased my awareness of numbers.

 I live with three small rescue dogs, and despite the disruptions to routine caused by my treatments, responsibility demands that I don't stop attending to them. "The person who cares for three dogs," I once wrote, "leads a dog's life." It's also true that anyone who cares for three parrots, toads, pots of plants, or children is not the master of his fate or the captain of his soul, as William Henley wrote in "Invictus." My hours are the dogs' hours. Throughout the day I put them outside and bring them back inside, beginning half an hour before I leave for Hartford. I do so again at 10:00 after their morning snack, at mid-day and mid-afternoon, at 5:00 following dinner, and later before they fall asleep. Unless the weather prevents her, on weekdays Vicki chaperones them on a stroll across the university campus. On weekends I join "the gang," and we walk along the Fenton River. People leashed to dogs have kennel vision. Many mornings at 7:15 as I drove home after my treatment, I spotted a gray man walking two Chihuahuas on the sidewalk bordering Charter Oak Avenue. Near the end of my appointments, I anticipated seeing him. The two dogs were old, and on cold days wore shabby coats. Better dressed is Coco a French bulldog whose owner walks her by my house at 8:20 just after I return home from Hartford. Coco has seven stylish coats including a rain slicker, a leather jacket, and my favorite, a black Halloween wrap decorated with orange bats.

    I am bothered when the dogs don't wag their tails, and I curry their favor and give them treats. At meals, Vicki and I talk about their habits, not my radiation regimen. Jack watches television and growls when other animals and malefactors appear. Unexpected noise bothers him. and if I drop a book, he leaves the room. Unlike Jack who prefers to nap alone in the study, Mia and Suzie trail after us, getting underfoot and tripping, causing me to bang against walls and clutch the corners of tables and dressers. Mia came to us from Texas and is too old to be molded by Connecticut home schooling. Men frighten her, and no matter how sweetly I wheedle, sometimes she hides and crouches under furniture when I call. Suzie has aged into a chorus of chortles, starting an hour before her dinner and continuing throughout the evening. Age has turned her into a foodie, and she begs as Vicki and I eat then afterward while Vicki straightens the kitchen. Later when I put her outside before bed, she importunes me for food, chortling, rubbing against my legs, and staring at me imploringly. All the dogs are senior pets, and Suzie suffers from canine senility. She is deaf and except when she is pursing food loses her way inside the house and out. We've imagined putting her to sleep for our convenience. However, imagined action rarely translates to deed, at least with family dogs. Like her predecessors Penny and Binky, Suzie will die at home in a bed beside the kitchen table. The difficulties of caring for Suzie, really nursing her, have made us aware of our characters and their inadequacies. Vicki and I now realize that we are not strong and selfless enough to care for an aged, needy relative. Fortuitously, we have few kin. Still each of us has a spouse. Vicki is lively and robust, but, as I sometimes think as I rub Suzie consolingly, Vicki's husband is being treated for cancer.

Driving is wearing, but life won't let me doze through hours in reclusive isolation. After reading my books, people write me. Their letters rouse and entertain. "You are an enigma—knowable when you write about Nature, otherwise not," a recent correspondent wrote. "I've tried to assign a percentage of truthfulness to what you write about Vicki, your wife. I've guessed anywhere from 0% to 80%. But one thing is clear. As you portray her, I've definitely always had a 'girl crush' on her. I just hope she brings you back to earth even half as much as you say." A young critic said he wanted to write about me and enclosed a page of probing questions. "If you must write about me," I responded. "study the Pickerings who appear in my books and forget the other Pickerings who have strayed beyond pages. In any case I don't know where most of these last are nowadays. Some are dead and likely are more comfortable in the grave than they were atop the ground. They won't take kindly to the spade, so leave them alone and let them rest in peace." My response ended the correspondence. "You are so prolific that long after you become food for nematodes, two-legged bookworms will gnaw your pages and read life into your name. I heard you have The Cancer and are knocking at the Door to Nehebkau's Den," a pedantic literary correspondent opined. "Mortality always depresses. But you are blessed. You will have an afterlife. How good that must make you feel." "Writing disappears faster than ice cream on a Mississippi sidewalk in July. The spot gleams for an hour, but then vanishes," I answered. "Will Allen Dromgoole died in 1934. She was almost sixty-five years old. During her life she wrote 13 books, 2 plays, an operetta, 8000 poems, and 5000 essays. In 1930 she was appointed Poet Laureate of the Poetry Society of the South. Most words are corpses almost before they are printed. Dromgoole and her pages moldered too quickly for last rites and today lie buried in a deaccession tomb in Potter's Field. Hers is the fate of all scribblers."

Several correspondents noted my interest in Nature. "Knowing how often you quote Wordsworth, I thought you'd enjoy this poem by St. John Emile Clavering Hankin," a man "buried" in Amarillo, Texas, wrote. Entitled "Lines," the poem was a parody of "The Tables Turned" which famously begins with the narrator telling his friend to quit his books and observe the natural world. I enjoyed the parody, two stanzas of which urged the studious desk-bound friend to: "Observe the linnet on the bough, / His note how clear and ringing! / His voice was mute at dawn, but now, / I notice, he is singing. / See how my dog comes running up / In answer to my whistle; / This flower is called a buttercup, / And that, I think, a thistle." I did not mention my treatments to neighbors in Storrs. In a small town even if people lop off their tongues and glue their lips together, news about ailments will out. "I heard that the devilish part that gets men in trouble when they are young and yet again when they are old is causing you to have radiation. Don't worry about it. You'll be fine," Susan wrote. "I had radiation several years ago. On me the target was higher up, aimed at the two things that get gals noticed when they are young and then cause them to be ignored when they start to droop."

More difficult than keeping health private is avoiding the winds of advertising. Among the solicitations that arrived at the house was one addressed to my Uncle Coleman urging him as a history buff to subscribe to *Vietnam Magazine*. A year's subscription cost $24 discounted from $41.94. As an incentive, if Coleman paid the fee within five days, he'd receive a pair of "Special Collectors" editions: *The Helicopter War* and *Great Last Stands of Vietnam*. Coleman was born in 1910. Because he appeared to be one hundred and ten, the Market Research Department of *Vietnam* must have assumed Coleman's reading days were limited. Consequently they urged him to mail his check immediately. To "beat the fast approaching deadline date!" the department wrote, showing a remarkably insensitive grave-side manner. Unfortunately for the subscription managers in Palm Coast, Florida, the solicitation arrived a couple of decades too late. Coleman died in Texas in 1997, 23 years ago. Afterward his mail came to Storrs.

Time has winnowed my acquaintances, and only rarely do I hear from former companions of school and place. I welcome their letters. Usually they are housekeeping correspondences describing who is moldering on a shelf in the basement and who is still puttering about in the kitchen spicing up life. Sometimes, they are bleak and dispiriting. "It is hard for me to lower my hopes," a friend informed me. *Hard* because my friend's hopes couldn't sink lower. Recently a doctor informed him that his daughter who had been mentally ill for several years would never get better. For a time electrical shock treatment had been beneficial, but it had stopped working. "Soon," the doctor, said, "she will have to be confined. No rehabilitation home can manage her, and medicine can't help her." On a happier note, a popular doctor in Carthage, Tennessee, celebrated his hundredth birthday. As a present an officer of the local utility called and said the doctor would never receive another fuel bill. "Those days are over." "He still drives," my correspondent wrote, "and plays a good hand of bridge." Invisible pictures painted by the eye of the receiver illuminate such letters, on this particular paper sketches of my Carthage, a windmill and a tobacco barn, strawberries, dark blue Iris, a tin roof, a one-arm well pump, a Persian cat named Scarlet, and on an oilcloth-covered kitchen table a cup of sugary coffee, the color that of sand, just right for a small boy.

    As people wrote me, so I thought about the characters populating my books. One evening Vicki and I talked about Peppy Whapadoo. Peppy was light-hearted and good natured and despite her name wasn't a flibbertigibbet. Around others she laughed spontaneously and effervesced eliciting smiles and encouraging people who were "out of sorts" to bask in consoling feelings of superiority. Never did she turn their assumptions to her advantage. "Peppy wasn't that kind of gal," Vicki said. She hid her intelligence under a bouquet of flowers—ordinary grocery-store chrysanthemums, red, yellow, and white rays of sunshine that burst out of vases and bucked up cooks confined to cramped kitchens. She befriended strangers and frequently appeared at back doors bearing cakes and casseroles. "Nice Peppy Whapadoo, Sweet Peppy Whapadoo," people said, patronizing her, bored because they couldn't discover any tainted morsels suitable for gossip in her character. "No serpent lurked in her garden," Vicki said, "and any that crept in would inhale the miasma of goodness and be so transformed, they'd pluck out their fangs with their tails, forswear hissing, and start purring."

Peppy had only one secret. Under the pen name Anna Quarium, she wrote popular mysteries. "The Fishbowl Series," a reviewer in the *Washington Post* dubbed them. Among her many titles were *The Loach Nest Monster*, *The Kissing Gourami's*, a steamy tale of jealousy and adultery; *The Ick*, in which a vial containing deadly bacteria is stolen by rogue CIA agents from a chemical-warfare laboratory beneath St. Paul's Cathedral in London, and *When the Lights Went Out* describing attempts to nab the kidnappers of four celebrities whose names had long appeared in neon on billboards above Broadway. Especially well-received by older readers was *The Angel Fish Murders* which followed a cyanide-hearted nurse as she glided from nursing home to nursing home, "breaking the chains binding the old and the tired to dementia." Peppy's most acclaimed creation was her detective Serendipitous Guppy. A litigious literatus accused Peppy of plagiarism asserting that Guppy's resemblance to Dorothy Sayers's Lord Peter Wimsey was too close to be an "innocent coincidence." Critics are addicted to reading between lines and ignoring headers, footers, and margins. Lord Peter and Guppy were spawned in different pools. While Lord Peter attended Eton and Balliol and was an English toff, Guppy was educated in the school of street corner vice. "To convict a larcenous ambulance chaser, I once audited a class in Harvard Law School," he said. "All I got out of it was two cramps, one in the head, the other in the backside."

All volumes featuring Guppy are entertaining, but my favorite is *Guppy to the Rescue*. In this he travels, among others, by skateboard, glider, military transport, and a tramp freighter manned by Indonesian pirates. He also rides sundry four and two footers, including a camel, a zebra, a farm-raised ostrich, and a tame kangaroo. Accompanying him is his secretary and sometime side and bed kick, Red Molly, whose hair is so bright that when she walks into bars owners douse the lights and fearful toppers call fire departments. In *Rescue* she and Guppy solve an unsolvable mystery and save the unsavable, the complications of which Vicki forbade me to describe lest I spoil the book for mystery aficionados. However, revealing one detail won't undermine the pleasure of reading and should whet the appetite of devotees of mystery and adventure novels. In the tale Guppy masters quick-change and appears in different disguises in every chapter, leading another critic to accuse Peppy of lifting Guppy's wardrobe and character from Sir Peter Blakeney, Baroness Orczy's Scarlet Pimpernel.

Critics seek sources here. They seek them there. They seek them everywhere. To give a single example, countless versions of Cinderella exist. It is a cliché of criticism that academics ambitious to establish themselves in children's literature unearth lost manuscripts. In an article published last month in an on-line journal, a critic discovered "yet another" Indian rendering of the tale. In this account from Uttar Pradesh, the mice the fairy god mother changed into the horses that drew Cinderella's chariot were originally Indian Star Tortoises. The carapace of the Star Tortoise is black. Rising across it are areolae or small lumps. They look like tiny mountains covered with yellow snow. From them thin yellow lines radiate and fall down through the black like streams. In this newly discovered version the god mother is not a fairy or a mother but a Sadhu, a holy man. After the Sadhu anoints the tortoises with water from the Ganges, they become giant black warhorses while the yellow streams become golden harnesses.

Let me dismount from my literary hobbyhorse, if that is possible for someone my age. As April showers bring spring flowers, so fall rains make householders worry about winter and the deleterious effects of snow and ice. The coronavirus has kept Mormons and Jehovah's Witnesses away from the door. It has not, though, muffled the doorbell. Fall is the season of roof and chimney gypsies. Shysters thrive in overcast weather and take advantage of the concerns of aged homeowners. "I was in the neighborhood repairing a chimney. Winter is coming, and I don't want anyone to suffer chimney problems. Your chimney looks good, but I'll be glad to inspect it for free just to insure that all is well," the pitch begins. Of course, all is not well. "I noticed your roof while I was on the way home from a job. There may be a problem," the second pitch begins. In this case the miscreant wheedles his way into the attic to inspect the roof from below. To create the appearance of integrity, he insists that someone in the house accompany him. Once in the attic, he diverts his companion's attention. While the person is looking elsewhere, the gypsy pours a container of water over a trunk or on a mattress, thus enabling him to discover proof that the roof leaks. "I'm embarrassed to reveal how much

I lost," a friend wrote. "But it was over eight thousand dollars." As could be expected, my friend was eighty-nine years old. Winter is old brain, not ice, phishing season. The bait varies, but last December using her debit card to buy gift cards cost an eighty-six-year-old acquaintance eleven thousand dollars. "I thought I was helping poor people in California. I gave the crooks my bank account number after they promised I'd be reimbursed," she told a detective. "California is a switching yard. The money went to thieves in India," the detective replied. At the moment radiation has not affected my judgement, and I am immune to scams. Alas, immunity weakens as a person ages, however.

Occasionally when I am at my desk, my pencil sinking in the soggy half of a compound sentence, I'll answer the telephone. "Maybe the call will shock me out of ineptitude," I think, "and I can vault onto a bony archipelago of dry sentences." "Is this Samuel?" a caller began on Wednesday. "Yes, Samuel it is, and what is the subject of this interruption?" I said in the snootiest intonation I could muster. The tone did not deter the caller. "I am phoning from the headquarters of New England Health Care," she said, "and how are your sore legs and swollen ankles today?" When I replied that I wasn't plagued by either podalgia or radiculopathy, she paused for a moment then scurried up my anatomy. "And how is the pain in your back?" she asked. "The only pain I'm experiencing is in my ass," I said. "You are the source of that, and I don't need to sign up for another health plan to cure it." With that I clapped the receiver back into its cradle and then divided the troublesome compound sentence into two workaday simple sentences.

Actually, winning the lottery wouldn't make me

cagier and more distrustful of others than I am now. When Social Security begins, wise people jettison waking dreams. Nighttime dreams are safer. Last week, I dreamed about my great friend Bill Weaver. Bill died in 2007, but in the dream his spirits were high, and we laughed and talked as we had in elementary and high school, college, and for forty years thereafter. One moment we were running through the surf in Florida, the next in Tennessee slapping each other on the back and cooking hamburgers. Sadly, in daylight the dead are not so lively while the quick are frequently too glibly alive to become trustworthy companions. Of course, there are exceptions. No longer do the antics of the corporate and pedagogical castes interest me, and the only newsprint I peruse "religiously" appears on the obituary page. During my radiation regimen several people I knew flickered out, and mutual acquaintances mailed me their obituaries. A few transformed death rattles into laughter and brought people back to life. A friend from my graduate school years in New Jersey died in in September, and one of his colleagues sent me the obituary. For forty years my friend taught economics at a mid-western university, and details of his career swelled the obituary like chicken feathers in a pillow. But then, his wife told me on the telephone, "Henry our son composed the account. It was an exercise in dutiful devotion. I wrote only one line: 'He was on too many committees.'"

Time, perhaps in conjunction with the radiation, or just maybe the darkening season, has tarnished recent weeks. One afternoon after a deluge of in-the-know emails preaching doctrinal purity, I decided to wash the English Department out of my mind. Although as a retiree I no longer had an office,

I'd kept a slot in the mail room, and once every six weeks I checked my mail and visited teachers whose names I had not forgotten. I wrote the assistant overseeing the main office during the coronavirus and told him to peel my name from the box in the mail room. "Forward or preferably throw away any mail I receive," I wrote. In truth nowadays I receive little mail at the university, and most people who were my colleagues are dead or almost so. The few who remain have moved out of town and simultaneously out of thought. Moreover, my affection for books has always been more personal than intellectual, or political. I cleared my own path through libraries, not because I was ornery but because I have always been a pedagogical loner. The word mentor was not in my vocabulary. I had no appetite for corpuscular pietism and didn't teach to persuade but to please myself. I wanted students to enjoy reading and appreciate life. I hoped they'd realize they could choose rewarding lives, but I did not indoctrinate. I was and am happily and selfishly old school and as such, as a critic put it, "a ghost from a bygone classroom. Not even an expert in unveiling the paranormal could restore you to academic attention."

On weekends I sleep until seven o'clock, and Vicki and I roam the woods along the Fenton River. The walks are familiar and reassuring. The muted damp aroma of fall wafts up from the soft churn of leaves, mostly hickories, oaks, and birches. Witchhazels have dropped their leaves, and their branches have burst into streamers of yellow flowers. Cold makes our skin tingle and sweetens the tart fruits of autumn olive. Needles transform the ground around white pines into dusty gold shags. On the forest floor mushroom blooming has slowed leaving blue fragments lingering here and there. A hermit thrush naps on a stubby limb and doesn't fly when we approach. Water is low, and the river is a quarry of marbled stones. Small blue asters gather in joyous congregations along our path. Green patches of hay-scented ferns mend the ground where deer have cropped the understory. Late one afternoon as I studied a turtle sunning on a rock exposed after the beaver pond dried, a cherry-faced meadow hawk landed on my shoulder. Most dragonflies had disappeared, and the meadow hawk was so exhausted it perched on me. "Who is it?" I asked Vicki. "My family has been dead too long for the methane and hydrogen sulfide released by putrefaction to fuse and fly up out of the grave." "Maybe it's your spirit," Vicki said, "a weary fall presence a little flush from radiation. Whatever it represents is unsuitable for a tattoo. A fall cricket would become you better. Amid the melancholy of the gray fields, they remain chipper and continue to sing." "How clever," I said. "Not clever," Vicki replied, "fitting."

Early Quakers believed that within each person was the presence of God or an inner light. Its beams revealed and directed people toward hallowed behavior, that is, loving one's neighbor as one's self and acting morally in social and governmental matters in accordance with the Sermon on the Mount. In his Journal John Woolman said that the love of money and worldly wisdom obstructed "the shining of the light of life into the soul." As a result, men could not "discern the good and perfect will of God." Popular gospel songs express similar thoughts. "Precious Lord take my hand," the song by the same name implores. "Lead me on, let me stand. / I am tired, I'm weak, I am worn. / Through the storm, through the night /

Lead me on to the light." "I saw the light, I saw the light," *I Saw the Light* declares, "No more darkness, no more night." "Just like a blind man I wandered alone. / Worries and tears I claimed for my own. / Then like the blind man that God gave back his sight / Praise the Lord, I saw the light." Would that the radiation I am receiving were metaphorical as well as actual. Would that besides burning cancer, it reduced unethical behavior to ashes. How fine it would be if it were a moral beacon clearing a path through the weeds and thorn trees of life, perhaps a little dimmer than the everlasting light that beamed upon the evangelist Phoebe Palmer as she "entered the highway of holiness" promulgating the doctrine of human perfection. Certainly, disease and radiation alter people, deathbed repentance reflecting that change, as well as being, my skeptical friend Josh says, "a supine last-minute hedging of bets."

I've never envisioned an inner light. Even in Stygian moments I do not wish to glimpse such a light. Although illusions can appear to illuminate, they are as real as the will-o'-the-wisp. I avoid and don't trust people who claim that the numinous or fanciful abstractions inspire them. I prefer the results of work to testimonials crediting inspiration. I enjoy gospel songs. But liking is not belief. Aside from stockpiling term life insurance when my children were young and amassing money enough to guarantee that Vicki's final decades are comfortable, I have thought little about my mortality. "Think of the radiation as a wake-up light," Josh said, having heard me mention John Woolman. In truth the light of awareness is waxing unbearably stronger. Vicki is twelve years my junior. When we married, I didn't consider the age difference. Now I cannot escape it.

"Was it right to marry a younger woman?" I fret. "Am I guilty of an unconscionable disservice? Have I condemned a lovingly-decent person to years of diminished living, her inescapable companion, an ailing querulous husband, a jailer more than a spouse?" Almost all our acquaintances are my age. Many have, as P. G. Wodehouse put it, gone through the gate in the garden wall, while the remainder, in grimmer, more accurate words, are trudging toward the abattoir. "Will my death, sentence Vicki to the shadow life of an undeserved solitary confinement? Her love deserves much better."

I suspect radiation will make me radio-active, with the emphasis falling on active. Perhaps my appreciation of natural outer lights will glow, and with renewed intensity, I'll gather wildflowers, birds, trees, creepers and crawlers, the not-me's that foster happiness and contentment. On our walk this past weekend the sight of a grand red oak almost brought Vicki and me to our knees. "It's a temple," Vicki said. Nearby a burl bellied out from the trunk of a white oak. "A dryad's seat," Vicki said. "Tread softly. This is Gaia's way," she added as burning bushes practically enclosed our path and the sunlight shining through their leaves made the ground and the air and ourselves bloom like damask roses. As for lesser medical matters, I haven't thought much about them. A couple of weeks ago, I asked the radiologist what would happen after my treatments ended. I wondered if he'd continue to see me or refer me back to the urologist who recommended him. "We'll kick you back and forth for a while," he said, "and if you're still around after three years, we'll send you on your merry way." Good sense, I thought, and we both chuckled.

Along with sense, good nature flourished at

the Center. The Friday before Halloween, Meagan a technician wore a unicorn headdress topped by two wiggly ears. After my treatment, she offered me candy from a "Trick or Treat" basket. Meagan is skilled and kind. "Real sweetener, not aspartame," another patient said. "Yes," I said and silently quoted Ella Wilcox's famous lines: "Sing, and the hills will answer; / Sigh, it is lost on the air. / The echoes bound to a joyful sound, / But shrink from voicing care." I rarely eat candy, but I chose a Snickers bar. "When you complete the 43 appointments," Vicki said later after she ate the Snickers, "I trust you'll receive a diploma and graduate Magna Cum Prostatae." The day following graduation, I have an appointment to have my teeth cleaned. Each year, the hygienist suggests that x-rays be taken of my teeth. Although I say "no," my response always sounds indecisive. This year "no" will be emphatic.

This morning I had my 43rd and last radiation. Daylight savings time ended this past weekend, and halfway through my final two drives to Hartford, the horizon turned blue then gray. No longer did I feel lost in the dark. The lights of approaching vehicles stopped resembling mines that detonated on my windshield and broke into blinding fragments, compelling me to become a white-line, shoulder-of-the-road driver. In the half-light of day, I didn't fret about drifting off the asphalt and knocking over a mailbox. I saw potholes and sunken manhole covers and did not have to rely upon memory to avoid them. Of course, I didn't become worry free. Only the nature of my anxiety changed. "How terrible it would be to crash during my last trip to Hartford," I said to Vicki yesterday. "It's so terrible it is bound to happen." Sleep did not banish the thought from my mind, and so I got up at 3:05. I didn't return to bed. "Jesus," I thought as the hours passed, "I'm probably going to fall asleep at the wheel."

When I arrived at the Center, Carol was waiting for me at the entrance. In her right hand was a carry-all overflowing with bags of cat food. In her left she held a card and a small lavender box with a blue ribbon pasted to the lid. Inside were two pumpkin muffins from Dunkin' Donuts, "for you and your wife." "Congratulations! You have made it through all of your treatments as of today!" Carol wrote, and "Thank you for your kindness and generosity for the donation to the 'feline fund.' Your contribution will keep him fed for weeks. Wishing you good health, happiness and all good things as you move forward on your journey. We will miss you in the AM." Carol signed the card "The Bench Club" and drew a heart. The *we* and the club were the nurses and the technicians who like me arrived in the morning before the door to the Center opened.

To say that I enjoyed my experiences at the Center probably makes me seem foolish. But in truth the appointments enlivened my days and made the hours of social distancing less viral. When I left the radiation room after my final treatment, the men in the waiting room applauded. I did a little dance, jitterbugging as well as an old guy can, and they cheered and laughed. The technicians wished me farewell and gave me a printed broadsheet signed by the personal at the Center. Outside the Center waiting for me and ignoring the cold unseasonable wind was Frank. He finished his treatments two weeks earlier, and he returned "to say goodbye and wish you all the best. Maybe we'll meet again." "That would be nice," I answered. When I got in my car, I sat for a while. "Damn," I said aloud then started the engine.

At noon Vicki and I walked to Dog Lane Café, drank coffee, and ate the muffins. Today is election day, and Sierra, a waitress, worried about the results. She said that militias frightened her. "Don't think about them," I said. "I grew up surrounded by militias. No member ever bothered me. I saw them often at the country club. Their uniforms made spotting them easy. When going into battle, they wore polo shirts with insignias sewed on the left-breast pocket, usually zoo animals like alligators and bears. Their fatigue pants were generally bright Madras or Palm Beach slacks, green and pink being the preferred colors of the latter. Yes, they were well-armed. Almost all carried golf clubs or tennis rackets." After finishing our coffee, Vicki and I strolled to Price Chopper. I bought a lottery ticket. On the Periodic Table of Elements, I am 79, Au or gold. Unless the table is science fiction, before the end of the year I should pocket a bar of gold.

Once I reach 80, I'm determined to break the lottery habit. On the table, however, eighty is mercury, and that creates a slight problem. Quicksilver is another name for mercury. Metaphorically, lottery winnings would be quick silver, money appropriate to my eightieth year and not earned by disciple and hard work—shucks! Three days ago, Vicki bought a bottle of Champagne. "To celebrate the end of your treatments," she said. "Maybe that will be a trifecta day. The half-life of the radiation will decrease. We'll win a million dollars in the lottery, and the mongrel in the White House will lose the election." "If he wins," I said, "I will howl and the Champagne will turn to vinegar." Vicki said she'd invent a mosquito drone, arm it with a Novichok, program it to seek hair soaked in tanning lotion, and release it near the sixteenth green on the International Golf Course at West Palm Beach. Once the drone located the target and pierced its skin, it would self-destruct in ten seconds, "making tracing the mosquito's original mission impossible," Vicki said.

    It's now after midnight. I'm going to bed. I should have been asleep three hours ago. Growing old in an old person's home is fatiguing. Although I no longer must wake at 4:30, the stairs are still getting steeper. Cracks wrinkle across the ceiling, and liver spots continue to stain the walls. I don't know the result of the election, but the Champagne left an acidic aftertaste, and at 11:00 not a single number on our lottery ticket was drawn. Sunday and Monday were windy and rainy. Trestles of limbs are scattered across the yard, and leaves are ankle high. Adjusting to an absence of schedule will be gradual. Still I'll continue to get up early. Tomorrow morning before the ground dries, I must start blowing leaves. The weatherman predicted that the week ahead will be cold, but that doesn't matter because sugar maples haven't dropped their leaves. The trees glow like torches, flashing orange and yellow, amber and lemon, so bright they'll warm the days. They'll quicken my spirits and shore up my back. Shouldering the leaf blower will be easy, and by evening I'll be tired and content, ready to eat dinner with Vicki in the study and watch "One Royal Holiday," a Hallmark Christmas movie.

Everything

"Nothing" is a more accurate title than "Everything." Actually, "Nothings" would be better, that is, if a nothing or emptiness can be plural. In any case in this essay I describe the miscellaneous and insignificant events in my orderly life. Late most afternoons, I put two folding chairs and a small table in the driveway, just the blind for Hallmark environmentalists, and Vicki and I sit and have tea. We eat banana bread or cupcakes. We watch the street, and I often ask Vicki if she likes the color of a passing car. Usually she doesn't. Occasionally passersby wave at us. We wave back, but because our eyes are weak, we rarely identify anybody. We chat quietly. One afternoon we watched a squirrel move her young from a nest in a red maple to new accommodations in a shagbark hickory. She crossed the drive near our feet but paid no attention to us. Not far from where we sit is a bird bath. Our presence does not alarm small visitors, not even skittish nuthatches. Elsewhere days are not so somnolent.

"Life is short," my cousin Buster wrote recently from Missouri. His neighbor Albert had a heart attack and died on a couch in his mother's house across the street. Albert was 38, Buster's age. He had five children by different women. "I didn't get started till late, till I was 29," he told Buster, explaining, "I had to do my time first." Albert was a felon and "spent a decent spell in prison." Buster noted that Albert didn't take care of himself. He ate poorly, avoided exercise, drank, and smoked. He also had a stent in his heart. It had been put there during surgery to save his life after he was shot in the chest. He'd also been stabbed, this before Buster met him and when he was "running with a bad crowd." On one occasion the local SWAT team burst into his mother's house looking for him. "There were probably more than a few people who wanted him dead," Buster recounted, adding that shortly before he moved across the street from Albert's mother, her house had been shot at in a drive-by shooting. One of the bullets struck the refrigerator as Albert and his mother sat nearby at the kitchen table. Albert co-existed in the house with his mother and her husband Fred, an "untrustworthy" drunk. Under the influence of alcohol Fred had "done something with a five-year old" that led to his being convicted as a sex offender. Albert despised Fred and did not care for his sister Zenda. She dropped by the house most days, but Albert said she was sour. Recently Albert and his mother had a fight that brought police to the door. Albert complained that his mother didn't do "shit" for him. He told Buster that he'd seen his father occasionally but had "never spoken a word to him." Albert had a second sister living in Florida and a brother "doing life plus 30."

"Albert had a lot of repressed rage," Buster wrote. "I always gave him a wide berth and made sure never to disagree with him except during mindless sports chatter. He wound up liking me and said I was the best neighbor he ever had." Albert wanted his own place, but because he was a felon, he couldn't find a rental. "He really needed to be alone, for himself, for everyone." "Albert had no future," Buster concluded. "To judge by the response to his death, he had worn out his welcome. He was abrasive, moody, touchy, unreliable." Because they had to be careful around him, "everyone was wary of him and perhaps he was wary of them, too. He had nowhere to go, nothing to do, and not much to offer." Albert's death was the third death in three years "on the short segment" of Buster's street. "Albert was a fixture on the street, and I saw him almost daily," Buster wrote, verbally shrugging his shoulders, "but now he moves on."

After reading Buster's letter to Vicki, I paused for a moment before saying, "a world apart." "Far apart," Vicki said agreeing, "a lifetime apart." I then changed the subject to my morning at Radiation Oncology at Hartford Hospital. When I was stretched out beneath the eye of the Trilogy machine, trousers unbelted and shirt pulled up, a young technician-in-training skipped into the room. "Hi," she gushed leaning over me, "my name is Caddy. How are you feeling today?" "Hi, Caddy," I said. "How nice of you to ask. I'm fine and am having a nice day. I hope you are having one, too." As I talked, I glanced at the wall on my right. Against it stood a sturdy rack similar to those in clothing shops. Instead of H. Freeman suits, body molds hung on the rack, much of the gear for men form-fitting from the waist down, for women, from the mid-drift up. Not everything in Radiation Oncology smacked of a haberdashery. Some sights were the salty matter of tears. Pasted to walls outside treatment rooms were posters. In the middle of the posters appeared hand-drawn calendars, twelve by ten for one month, two months twice that size. Above each calendar curving in a rainbow of colors across the poster was the name of a young patient, all that I saw boys, Henry, Jack, and Adrien. Below each day of the month was a large postage-stamp sized square. In the squares nurses pasted stickers bright with cartoon characters, a new sticker each time the child came for treatment. On the margins of the posters surrounding the calendars, kindly attendants drew animals and super-heroes, among the latter, Captain America, Spiderman, and The Hulk, among the former, llamas, turtles, elephants, camels, and zoos of cuddly reassuring pandas.

I didn't mention the posters to Vicki. They would have made her melancholy. For me, body molds, the bubbly girl, and radiation were simply appointments of daily living. For parents of the children, the posters were sad harbingers of loss and lives unlivable. On the death of his son the Japanese poet Kobayashi Issa wrote a haiku. "The world of dew / Is the world of dew. / And yet, and yet—," the yet's, not for the self but for others and the shadows that inevitably fall across families. They are unsuitable complements of afternoon teas and the momentary lightness of being. The truth is that among the many nothings of the everyday lurk burdensome somethings. If one lifts the curtain of green leaves wrinkling over the end of his driveway, he'll become of aware of dewy evanescence and notice sights that, as Wordsworth put it, lie too deep for tears.

Most of Vicki's and my afternoons are driveway hours. They are calm, and although we are aware of misery, sun and rain sweeten the air. The Sunday after receiving Buster's letter Vicki and I ate breakfast at Spring Hill Café. We eat there often and always order "The Alarm Clock": two eggs over light, sourdough bread, patty sausage, and coffee, each cup a blend of regular and decaffeinated. We sit at a table under the menu written in chalk on a wall beside us. Vicki faces the door, and I, the wall behind the bakery counter.

Painted on it is the logo of the café, a doughnut partly encircled by the words "Spring Hill Café." In the doughnut hole sits a brown coffee cup. From the top of the cup rises a sunflower blooming in a lather of yellow. In one of his forgotten poems, John Trotwood Moore laments, "O Voices that long ago left me, / O eyes that were long ago bright, / How often you come when the shadows / Creep into the eyes of night."

Moore was genially sentimental but wrong. For the elderly the eyes of old friends don't shine through the years. Neither do their voices pulse like doorbells. Age erases the past. At breakfast Vicki and I chat about momentary nothings, two weeks ago our dog Suzie's sickening herself by eating hickory nuts blackened by fungus and then Jack's and Mia's fear of thunderstorms. Jack flees upstairs and crouches under the bed in Eliza's old room while Mia hides in the kitchen. Vicki lowers the door of the dish washer, and Mia buries herself beneath it. Vicki and I do not mention political matters. Our bread would mildew and our eggs addle. We'd gnash our teeth and be unable to chew. We chat about happier things, often words, recently "Jenny with Many Feet," an old colloquial phrase for a centipede, and then puddocks, a name for toads still heard occasionally. During the meal we usually bring up something we've read appropriate to the moment, most recently Gilbert Allen's poem "The Woman Who Vacuums Her Driveway." Eastern Connecticut has sunk into a drought, and hickories are raining nuts in ground-thumping torrents. The far end of our drive is awash with shattered nuts, making walking hazardous. "Anyone who ventures down the drive is liable to roll an ankle," Vicki said. "I wish we could hire that woman to vacuum our drive every afternoon before the newspaper and the mail are delivered."

Occasionally we season our sausage and bread with an oddity, on this past Sunday a link to Samuel and Erica Pickering's Wedding Website. A casual acquaintance who wondered if I was related to "the happy couple" sent the link to me. The kinship was nominal not corpuscular. My offspring are quick, but all my other Pickering relatives are dead. In the photograph attached to the link, Samuel and Erica sat on a sofa on the shoulder of a garden path. The sofa was upholstered in velvet and bound to the frame and arms by gold braids. Planted on the ground behind the sofa were hostas and lamb's ears. Samuel and Erica gazed at each other and looked amiable. Both held a bottle of Modelo beer. I once drank Modelo with dinner. But because the bottles were so squat that twisting and pushing were necessary to fit them into beer socks, Vicki stopped buying them. At my age, chances were better that I was related to Ambrose Bierce's "An Obituarian" than to the newlyweds. The subject of Bierce's poem specialized in graveyard verse. "Death-Poet Pickering sat at his desk," the first stanza began, "Wrapped in appropriate gloom; / His posture was pensive and picturesque, / Like a raven charming a tomb."

Only rarely do we notice other people in the café. One morning a woman didn't simply talk with her mouth full. She stored breadcrumbs in her cheeks then shouted spewing them out like acorns blown from oaks during a high wind. The sight brought to mind "Refinement," a chapter in Wilhelmina FitzClarence Munster's *My Memories*, an etiquette book that has long entertained me. Of a wordy masticator, Munster complained, such a person "will talk with his mouth so distended by food, which for conversational convenience he stows away in some mysterious receptacle which he apparently possesses somewhere inside his cheeks that he reminds one of some wild beast surprised during its meal, the principal difference in the likeness being that whereas the wild beast would probably run away, the other individual alas! doesn't."

After breakfast this week Vicki bought a "for the road" doughnut and a loaf of zucchini bread from the bakery at the café, and we hurried away before a member of the woman's gastronomical tribe appeared. Next, we walked along the Fenton River for two and a half hours, tiring ourselves and the dogs. Before going home, we drove to Willington and at Wright's Orchard purchased a basket of peaches. To recuperate from the odyssey, we had tea in the driveway near the house but far from the torrents of nuts. Vicki divided the doughnut and submerged each half under whipped cream and a thick ledge of peach slices.

On walks Vicki and I stroll. I've become shaky. No longer am I surefooted enough to cross streams skipping from one wobbly stone to another. On paths I study the ground to forestall catching my shoes on the roots of hemlocks breaking through the dirt like varicose veins. Almost all we notice is familiar. "The walker does not need a large territory," John Burroughs wrote. "The walker has the privilege of the fields, the woods, the hills, the by-ways. The apples by the roadside are for him, and the berries, and the spring of water." Although the things Vicki and I see are insignificant, they transform our passings into gladsome somethings. Like magic dust they waft through minutes and brighten the hours. The neverending changes of years and seasons don't bring the transitory nature of being to mind. Instead they make one aware of constancy. Newness becomes part of continuance and slips seamlessly into paths worn by previous walks. In early September Japanese knotweed bloomed. Blossoms sprayed out of the ends of twigs, individual flowers icy white and sharp looking like crystals. The tall stems of mugwort cascaded over in minty ponytails. Horseweed turned sparse and scratchy. Here and there seed heads turned so white they seemed yellow. Summer's chase had ended, and giant foxtails lagged lethargically.

The flower stalks of Joe-Pye weed and boneset dried and looked like soiled dishrags. The stems of vervain curved slump shouldered, and flower spikes resembled the tines of wooden rakes stored in a backhouse and forgotten. Fruits on dogwood were gun metal blue, and those of autumn olive had begun to darken into burgundy. Festive strings of virgin's bower wound through dogwood teasing and wrapping the berries in silk. The hips of multiflora rose had collapsed and blackened. While ragweed flourished, nettles drooped enervated and stingless. At the edge of a field, wind shook the crowns of poplars creating a high metallic crinkling. Leaves of black birch had turned yellow and slipping from trees drizzled through the air in trembling curves. Along a shoulder of a sandy road bushy heath asters bloomed in white tangles. I crushed a handful of pussy toes. The fragrance is weak, and most people don't detect anything, but to me the blossoms smelled like licorice sprinkled with all-spice.

On the sunny lip of the beaver pond, barnyard grass was bristly and unshaven, while smartweeds were boudoir pink: lady's thumb, Pennsylvania, and marsh pepper. Vicki and I sat above the pond on the sharp side of a hill. The pond had dried into a mud flat splotched by small puddles. The sides of the puddles rapidly closed over the water like eyelids. Even so a green hero pinched small fish out of the puddles, and two solitary sandpipers plucked worms from the mud. Occasionally the resident kingfish rattled over the beaver lodge travelling to and from the Fenton River. A platter of mushroom grew besides us on the hillside. White and sunken in the center, they leaned over in a side saddle tilt. They may have been russula's, milk-white brittlegills, or perhaps a lactarius, peppery milkcaps.

    Vicki and I chatted and rubbed our dogs as we sat on the hill. The dogs are old, and they no longer scamper and sniff as they once did. Suzie suffers from dementia, and caring for her is exhausting. If we don't leash her, she wanders off and becomes lost. She is deaf and cannot hear us calling. To find her, Vicki stays in place while I jog trails with which she is familiar. "Tending to a relative with Alzheimer's must be impossible," Vicki mused. "Maybe it was easier when people lived on farms in extended families." "Last week I talked to a woman who gave up a job she loved and nursed her mother for twelve years," I said. "If the radiation fails, I promise not to malinger. I won't wreck the lives of you and the children." "Oh, Sam, please," Vicki said. "Don't talk about things that will break our hearts." "Reason not the reason," I replied and urged Vicki to look beyond the beaver pond, across the cattails, and over the alders. The meadow was a yellow cloud of goldenrod glowing and smothering brambles, scrubbing and altering the landscape. At first glance the goldenrod so transformed the end of the meadow that it seemed to demonstrate the ephemeral nature of everything. Later, however, as I looked and thought longer, appreciation rooted and grew, and the flowers seemed a sign of enduring vitality. Vicki said that although the goldenrod was lovely, she missed the milkweed that had once flourished in the meadow. "Only a few stems remain. I loved the pink balls, the bumblebees, the caterpillars, the monarch butterflies, and the teardrop pods, their silky seeds weeping and sailing into the air. Remember when we used to open the pods and shaking the seeds over each other laughed and danced about?" "Yes," I said, "that was something, really, really something, almost everything."

Solstice Sunshine

December storms into Connecticut mounted on the back of gunny gray clouds bringing Jack-in-the-Box rains and guttural roaring winds. Culverts plug and overflow, and trees scream and toss limbs. Pillows of snow fall, and for a day or two the world glistens and seems a softer place. But then the melt begins, and the snow turns to ice that jerks a person's feet from under him and seems alive and malevolent. After ice comes mud, slushy but so bent on getting into the house that it appears willful, intent on marking floors—stairs, tables, chairs, desks, all things against which clothes can conceivably brush. Along with squally weather, December brings mailbags of letters. As the end of the year approaches, old companions from school and neighborhood slow for a moment and take stock. They write letters. Some serve as Christmas greetings and describe the doings of family. Others are simply letters written so, as correspondents say, "we won't lose touch."

In the past, such letters seemed out of season. They blossomed like spring and glowed with optimism as people and families budded with promise. The letters made it easy to ignore the growing dark and the diminishing daylight hours. When branches thumped the roof, I didn't worry about what would happen next, fearing that a costly repair was in the offing. I still receive letters in December, but I am older. My friends are fewer, and the mail pouch is lighter. No longer do friends rake leaves or clear snow from their driveways. They hire other people to do the work. Now most of the letters I receive are wintry and seasonal. As days close-in, so do lives, and people ponder ends. The promises of yesteryears have blown, and life has wilted. "Every winter I cross names out in my address book. I'm glad you are still here. You're still here—aren't you?" an elementary school classmate wrote. "Death," he concluded, "has become a nuisance. I rarely leave the house, and I don't miss people not even folks who were once dear friends. My days are emotionless, and I lack the energy to write letters of condolence, send flowers, and attend funerals. I'm too old to pretend any death matters to me. What matters are breakfast and dinner and the workings of my inner parts. Sam, I am simply deathed out."

"I no longer drive. My children demanded that I stop, and when I was slow to obey, they seized my keys," Johnny recounted. "I guess it is for the best, but I don't know if I can stand watching more television." "Life has been grim recently," Niles wrote. Rita, his stepdaughter, committed suicide by jumping off the Memphis-Arkansas Bridge. Recovering her body from the Mississippi took five days, and "Rita was not in open-casket shape when she was found." Rita was middle-aged and depressed. She couldn't bear to die alone, so when she jumped, she cradled her dog in her arms. "Writers are inquisitive," Niles wrote, "and so for the record, rather the funeral guest book, the dog was a Yorkshire Terrier. Rita named it Daughter, after, I assume, the child she never had. Daughter's body disappeared. If it had surfaced, I suppose Anne [Niles' wife] and I would have buried her in the casket with Rita, a bit macabre but Rita had no friends so there were no mourners to object. To forestall the sighs of animal lovers, I should add that Daughter had begun to suffer from Senior Dog Anxieties, trailing Rita from room to room clinging to her feet, and then at mealtimes becoming frantic and yipping." In the lives of many old people, pets take the place of absent friends and families. Niles's neighbor Henry Standish died in April. "His wife Marty died eighteen years ago," Niles wrote. The couple were childless, and for years Henry's closest companion was his cat. "It died a month before Henry," Niles wrote, "and I think grief killed Henry." On the face of Henry's tombstone are his and Marty's names, Niles continued. "Engraved on the back is 'Precious Pet More Than Loved. Dearest, Dearest Daffodil Pussy Willow Standish.'"

In stuffy younger years, I believed only names, biblical verses, and dates of birth and death should be carved on markers. Now I think personalized tombstones enliven graveyards. Almost exploding from many newer headstones are high relief sculptures. The most popular are athletic: foot, soccer, and basket balls. Reaching out and to the side of a monument in Florida to sweep through a backhand is a full-sized tennis racket, its strings not gut or nylon but a mesh of granite molded and wrapped around thin steel wires. In upper New York state a polo pony bounds out of the monument of a horse trainer. The sculpture is modeled on one of the horses raring and galloping across the frieze of the Parthenon. On the stone appear the pony's head, shoulders, withers, and front legs, these last bandaged to protect them from being hit by polo balls. Above, on the neck and muzzle are the bridle and the sundry straps used to control the pony, martingale and throat lash, among others. "This is the family Pegasus," a relative of the trainer told me. The pony's wings are not carved on the monument "but like real wings and poetry" lift the imagination, enabling viewers to post above "thoughts of loss and death."

From City Beach in Western Australia, Nigel wrote that he was watching the sunset. "If Janey were alive, she'd be sitting beside me, and we'd be listening to Patti Page singing 'Let Me Call You Sweetheart.' But she's dead, and I can't bear to hear to any of our old favorites, tunes like 'Boogie Woogie Bugle Boy,' 'Tuxedo Junction,' and 'Stormy Weather.' Whenever one comes on the radio, I turn the machine off." Beth telephoned to inform me that Rosey an elementary school classmate died. "She was," Beth declared, "one of those nice women about whom nothing bad can be said which is the worst thing that can be said about anybody." Classmates were on my mind, and I phoned Jake whom I hadn't seen since 1959 when we graduated from high school. Once he and I had been study buddies. Discovering Jake's whereabouts and telephone number took a morning, but I found him living with his daughter in Arizona. She answered the phone and handed the receiver to Jake. He greeted me ebulliently. Immediately he described a picture on the wall of the room in which we studied sixty years ago. "Golly," I thought, "what a fine memory." I thought too soon. He then told me that he did not take a single pill at breakfast. On my saying that he was fortunate not to have to swallow a medicine cabinet of pills every day, he asked, "What pills?" Afterward our conversation collapsed. Jake's sentences were garbled. His ideas drifted aimlessly, and he mentioned occurrences that never happened. Alas, I soon realized what was wrong. It was the same old, literally old, story of aging. Eventually, I gave him my email address, repeating it three times. Jake said he'd write me that night. His daughter then took the receiver and thanked me for calling saying hearing my voice meant "so much" to her father. As could be expected, Jake did not write.

"My vision is poor," Nelson wrote good-humoredly from Kentucky. "My hearing is poor. My balance is poor. My muscles have vanished. Two of my ribs are cracked. I walk with a cane, and I have fallen several times, two bloody, none fatal. But what the Hell—for someone eighty-six, I am in good health. I'll be in even better shape, skipping fettle, gay as an ogre after someone scoops up that piece of shit occupying the White House and dumps him into the sewer." Nelson taught history of the language, an occupation that colors his assertions—often making them bawdy or scatological. In October, he sent a letter to the opinion page of the *Advocate Gazette*, his local newspaper. He noted that statistics compiled by the American Mercantile and Mathematical Association revealed that inhabitants of politically red states purchased more toilet paper per capita than did inhabitants of blue states. "This is because people wearing scarlet *R's* have to wipe egesta out of their mouths several times a day." The paper did not print Nelson's letter. "Egesta is recondite, and I thought it might confuse the adolescent editor and cause her to lose the scent, so to speak," Nelson confided. "I should have masqueraded as an economist," he concluded, "and said that most inhabitants of red states were eighty to eighty-five cents short of a mental dollar." Attached to Nelson's letter was a photograph of him wearing a blue baseball cap. Printed on the crown in white letters was "Make Turnip Greens Great Again."

Almost all my correspondents swore off politics decades ago, and few mentioned soiling governmental matters. Even if they suddenly mustered the gumption to be outspoken, they were in the December of their lives. They knew their time had passed, and no one would pay attention to them. "I listened to Verdi all week, All that passion! That spontaneous life!" Charles a classmate at Sewanee wrote in the fall. "The operas brought old dreams to mind. After college I reduced everything to computation and made a pile of dough. It bought a lot of things which the kids appreciated, and which, I suppose, the grandkids will benefit from. But once upon a time, I wanted to accomplish something culturally. The life I imagined leading has always and only existed in draft form."

Of course, replying to the letters occasions my swallowing the truth and gulping down a pitcher of rose water in hopes of easing dissembling and making my words resemble those of a medicine show barker. Or as another correspondent wrote me, "On my desk awaiting an uplifting answer is a long letter from my roommate at Bowdoin. He is down in the dumps because he is old and like everyone our age has a slew of ailments. I don't know how to cheer him up. I'm not doing well myself and drumming up verve and enthusiasm for anything seems impossible. The train for Euphoria left the station several operations ago."

Thirty years ago, playpens of children and grandchildren filled letters. Now offspring are inconspicuous, the paragraphs devoted to their antics usurped by concerns about health. No matter the season, things would seem amiss if letters written by people my age did not mention Cancer. "THEY GOT IT ALL," Patricia wrote describing an operation for colon cancer, "all eleven inches of it." "I am now deep into what I once considered unreachable years," Terry said. "My new oncologist looks like she has just left her high school prom, but she thinks she can get the crab out of my bones. Strangely, I almost believe her. But God, I am tired of obsessively tending to my body. So many things in the world are more interesting. Sometimes I wake in the night and wonder why anyone should waste her time trying to resuscitate a carcass."

"Last New Year's Day, I packed the car for Florida," Terry wrote from Charlotte. "I didn't go far. The next morning I couldn't hear and my legs wouldn't work. Aside from trips to the hospital, I didn't leave the house until July. I spent most of that time in bed, dragging myself out only to go to the bathroom. I can walk now, but I'm unsteady and each excursion is perilous. Moreover I have bouncy eyes. Whenever I focus on something, it hops about like a Mexican jumping bean. In October, a doctor ran a series of blood tests and discovered I'd had the virus. He assured me that I would get better—slowly. Maybe I will."

For a week, the weather had been unpleasant, and I hadn't jogged. The day after reading Terry's letter, however, I ran in hopes of purging crabbiness from my carcass. The morning was icy, and a rough, uncivilized wind blew rain across the day in billowing, slapping curtains. I ran alone. My usual jogging companion David doesn't run on stormy days. Moreover, early that afternoon, he had an appointment with an ophthalmologist. That evening I wrote him saying running had been foolish. I said the weather had sunk to my bones and that I was still cold after drinking pots of tea, "The alternative to being cold, wet, and miserable like you," David replied, "is to be warm, dry, and miserable like me. Driving to, waiting, seeing, and returning from the doctor's office took four hours. Of those two hundred and forty minutes, I spent only seven with the grand man himself, and seven is an exaggeration. The actual number was six and a half."

Although Aldrich spent much of the year in an Intensive Care ward, he heisted himself off the operating table long enough to kick start his anesthetizing humor and close his letter with a good-natured tale. "Like me, timeworn but still stout," he said. Late one night after an evening of carousing, an old countryman stumbled into a tent meeting hearing the hullabaloo and thinking it caused by a girly show. He sat down on a bench just as the preacher was laying his hands on a "nubile piece of Whitman's Sampler." An elderly evangelical sister noticed the newcomer on the bench and approaching him pressed her palms around his right hand in prayer, "Brother," she said, "brother, do you love Jesus?" "Well, ma'am," the old man said, pondering and rubbing his stubbly chin with his free hand, "I can't go so far as to say I love him. No, I can't go so far as that. But, dadgumit, I'll say this—'I ain't got nothin' agin him.'"

Several correspondents deadened their pains for the page and sent insouciant letters, albeit shadows sometimes mitigated the humor. "I have spent much time pondering my obituary," Elbert wrote. "This fall I stopped attending football games. Instead, on Saturdays, I visited funeral homes in order to plan my backdoor exit. I don't want a cotton candy affair, just a workaday hot dog and popcorn au revoir." Enclosed in Elbert's letter was an obituary clipped from a newspaper in Massachusetts. "I've read so many obsequies that the 'Lord of the Divine Hall' should award me a Ph.D. in necrology," he said. "Because small minds are interested in the extraordinary and genius in the commonplace, I think you will enjoy this sample of local last quarter kick-off color." The clipping described the life of "Murray D," the D being not an abbreviation but Murray's middle name. Murray dropped out of school at sixteen and went to sea working on cargo ships. "When returning home from a voyage to the Caribbean," the obituary recounted, "Murray met the love of his life, his common law wife Betty." Trivia like diplomas and marriage licenses did not concern the fruitful pair. Betty and six of the couple's eight children, nineteen grandchildren, and six great-grandchildren as well Albert J, "Murray's four legged buddy" survived "Poopdeck Pappy" and wished him, as the obituary put it, "sunny days, palm trees, barrels of rum, and piles of pigs and coconuts."

Only one letter evoked a cynical guffaw. Madeline and I had known each other since kindergarten. We kept in touch through the decades, in part because her life was lonely and sad. Her only child died fifty years ago shortly after his son was born. She didn't remarry and devoted her days to raising her grandson. She had means and didn't stint the boy, overindulging his whims and sending him to expensive private schools, summer camps, and three or, perhaps, four colleges. Sadly, he did not repay her affection with love but cupidity. Madeline died in August, and her grandson and heir wrote me in December. "Knowing that MaMa M. has gone back home gives me great peace," he said. "Peace and pence," I murmured. "Because of the virus there was no funeral or graveside ceremony. Later, Raquel [his wife] and I intend to celebrate her passing on Turks & Caicos at a resort near Providenciales. We are taking her ashes with us. We have already packed them in a travelling bag along with pictures of my dear father and her favorite cat Mr. Hugh. We didn't want to stint on MaMa M.'s farewell so all three of us are staying in a penthouse suite. MaMa M. loved collecting sea shells and always wanted to go to the Caribbean. Isn't it wonderful that she can visit now? We know her spirit will accompany us wherever we vacation. I can see her kicking up sand and splashing water on Mr. Hugh."

I learned a few things. A man whose father knew my grandfather sent a clipping from an old newspaper. In 1935 Grandfather served as master of ceremonies at a memorial service held in the Carthage Cemetery to honor "Carthage's first settlers." Fite, Myer, Fisher, Pickering, McClarin, Swope, Garrett, Oliver, Cullom, McKee, Hale, Gardenhire were "recognized for their contributions to the history of Carthage." Grandpa was not the only Sam Pickering mentioned in the mail. A cousin whom I had not seen since 1957 wrote me. Sarah, her mother, had married Mother's first cousin. Now ninety-three and in a nursing home, Sarah had inexplicably become interested in my whereabouts, and she asked a fellow resident to find me on the Internet. The man found my address at the University of Connecticut and an obituary. This past year another Sam Pickering, Jr., a geologist, died in Georgia. "Mother is a little fuzzy," Sarah's daughter wrote, "She thought you lived in Florida and not Georgia. She remembered that you were always catching bugs and snakes, but she didn't think you became a geologist. Besides the names of Sam Pickering's parents in the obituary looked wrong. I assured mother that you might well be alive and promised to ferret you out above or in ground." Fog often blankets my memory, and like Sarah, I misremember. How alive, I wonder, are forgetful people? Among the stories told about St. Gregory of Aran is one describing his being beheaded by a tyrant in Connemara. Afterward Gregory grabbed his head and strode off to a sacred spring. There he washed the blood off his face, stuck his head back on his neck, and returned to his anchor hole in the Aran islands. Would that I could bathe my head in a holy spring. I'd scrub myself with steel wool and remove all traces of fuzziness so that never again would I worry about dementia. I'd even forget the word existed.

Only a single correspondence irked me, and the source of the irritation was not in the body of the letter but in the closing. Every year a childhood friend ends his letter writing, "I'm praying for you." The friend is faithful and decent, and his closing is habitual. It is reflexive and no more meaningful than "all the best." Still I experience a bilious acid reflux reaction when I see it. I realize that being irritated by such a small thing is petty, presumptuous, and simply asinine. Maybe scouring my head in a holy spring would oust such pettifoggery from my thoughts. Inconsistency makes my reaction to the valediction worse. In September, I wrote my friend. I enclosed a copy of a religious poem which I admired, Thomas Edward Brown's "My Garden" in which God is pantheistic rather than doctrinaire.

> A Garden is a lovesome thing, Got wot!
> Rose plot,
> Fringed pool,
> Fern'd grot—
> The verist school
> Of peace; and yet the fool
> Contends that God is not—
> Not God! In gardens! when the eve is cool?
> Nay, but I have a sign:
> 'tis very sure God walks in mine.

In the mail Vicki and I received the week before Christmas, surgeons donned Santa Claus scrubs and IV's disappeared behind wreaths. Hedges of holly grew along the margins of letters and cards. They turned the winter sky green and red and shielded families from witchcraft and unforeseen medical enchantments. As I looked at pictures on the cards, I momentarily forgot that what was given could and at some time would be taken away. On the front of Jeffrey's and Varina's card was a photograph of them, their children and their spouses, and a baker's assortment of grandchildren. Everyone wore white and was smiling, all wholesome and healthy. "Christmas cookies," Vicki said, "crescents covered with powdered sugar." From Portland, Bill mailed "Bill & Peg's Excellent Year," a broadside describing the high points of past twelve months. In the center of a Christmas wreath appeared a calendar. After each month appeared one or two short sentences chronicling Bill and Peg's activities. As could be expected from an account written by a bookish male my age, Bill's tone was wintry and more icy than snowy. His observations weren't fluffy and adolescent but were harder and slightly jaundiced and to oldsters immediately familiar, causing gusts of resigned laughter. "April: Asked strangers to pick out our groceries," the Calendar noted, "June: Learned how to work Zoom," "August: Said to Hell with the pandemic, and walked all the way to the mailbox," "September: Got fed up with Zoom and disappeared," and "December: Are hoping that millions of Americans ahead of us in line, will choose not to be vaccinated. Spread the word, vaccines are a plot to inject us with microchips." "Bill's year was more eventful than ours," Vicki said after reading the broadside

My old rowing companion Geoff sent a springtime card that belied his years. Inside a garden of fifteen pictures showed Geoff and his family: in Krakow last New Year's Day, skiing in Spain, playing golf in Tahoe, reading in a green, shaded garden in Sweden, and having a family meal in his home on the waterfront in San Francisco. In other pictures, grandchildren bounced basketballs, helped construct a school in Guatemala, played the piano, and danced in a ballet performed outdoors because of the virus. In one photograph family members congratulated a grandson on his being admitted to a prep school; in another friends paraded by in cars to celebrate a granddaughter's twelfth birthday. Vicki did not immediately show me the photographs because she thought they'd make me envious. She was wrong. The exuberance delighted me. "Aren't the pictures a little over the top?" she asked. "No, happiness buoys the spirits," I said. "They are the apples and oranges, the candy bars that make the heart's Christmas stocking bulge."

Although the tenor of the letters and cards was generally drearier than those received in the past, December itself was much the same. Titmice and chickadees gleaned the clapboard on the house. Blue jays flew caterwauling into the lilacs by the back door. Nuthatches scooted up and down hickories, and downy woodpeckers jumped nervously from branch to branch. A pair of pileated woodpeckers called to each other in the wood behind the house, and on afternoons when the sun shined like a chorus, Carolina wrens burst into gleeful accompaniment. Occasionally my old companion a red tailed hawk visited and perched on a limb outside my study. Fewer juncos than usual dug through the dead grass in the back yard, but the number of blue birds increased. Almost every day a flock of a dozen or so appeared in the yard. They landed on limber branches only slightly above eye level and fluttered about blue, orange, and white like small Christmas candies wrapped in tinfoil. When snows began to melt and bare spots spread across the ground, flotsams of robins appeared, sweeping in then ebbing and hyperactively bounding in all directions, not running across the grass in straight lines as they do in the summer.

In the middle of the month a deep snow fell, and the yard looked like a cartoon, as pure as wintry scenes on sentimental Christmas cards. The neglected woodpile ceased to crumble and became a white drift. Sheets of snow blanketed evergreens bending their limbs into elegant curtseys. Clerical collars wrapped branches on other trees making them so lovely they seemed holy. For two days I was yard bound, and the quiet isolation awakened physical, not anecdotal memories. A hank of snow lashed my face, its sting not sharp and cold but soft and summery buzzing like honey bees in clover. Cars vanished from nearby roads and the air was as fresh as the fragrance of early summer magnolias. When sunlight shined through crystals atop the downfall, the beams broke into red, yellow and blue, transforming the white surface into a woodland wayside of spring violets. In November a vixen refurbished an old burrow behind our house. On inclement days I supplemented the contents of her larder with dog food: "Chicken & Sweet Taters Recipe Bites," Kibble, small biscuits shaped like bones—treats which we give our packlet after long walks. Three or so times a week, I also gave her mice whose fondness for peanut butter made them careless, luring them into traps in the basement. Only rarely did I see the fox, but after the big storm, I saw her twice. The sight of her red coat glowing like embers on the white snow was lyrical.

Because it obliterated the landscape outside the house, the snow turned me inward into a sentimental fantasist, and I read Winifred Watson's *Miss Pettigrew Lives for a Day*, a wondrous accompaniment for cold nights, eggnog, and logs blazing in a fireplace. Because it is too strong for me now, I no longer drink eggnog, and because I worry about chimney fires, I haven't laid a fire in the house in thirty years. However, drab facts don't matter when a person is snowbound. The book was a fairy tale sparkling with social butterflies attracted to the light of night clubs and incapable of conversations other than the seductive and the silly—things serious people don't say but wish they had said when they read them on the page. The story was an enchantment gay with promiscuity and ending with "unvirtue" rewarded. It described the Cinderella-like transformation of Miss Pettigrew, a drab depressed governess into a stylish middle-aged seductress with a hardy, vigorous boyfriend. Guinevere Pettigrew was, Watson wrote at the beginning of the novel, a "rather angular lady of medium height, thin through lack of good food, with a timid, defeated expression and terror quite discernible in her eyes, if anyone cared to look." No one looked because "there was no personal friend or relation in the whole world who knew or cared whether Miss Pettigrew was alive or dead." She had never been kissed and would have been horrified by the demimonde, providing she'd heard of it.

As a person ages, he thinks less about the short future ahead than about the past. Indeed, the most propitious time to speculate about the future is after it has become the past. In any case, the oldster becomes a secular penitent. He regrets the times when he behaved acceptably and expediently and as a result missed the pleasures of insouciance and irresponsibility. From the perspective of many years his embracing what society deemed praiseworthy often seems weak conformity, a betrayal of life when he should have fluttered like a butterfly and alighting on weedy blossoms basked in the sun and waggled his wings. Thus when Miss Pettigrew broke out of her smothering pupal shell and took flight, my imagination leaped in unison. In 1938 when the book was published no one would have said, "you go, girl." Although too slangy for my taste, the remark seemed appropriate as I sat in the study and dreamed through cold evenings. I wondered why I had not walked out of the classroom years ago when I heard William Roscoe sing, "Come take up your hats, and let us away in haste, / To the Butterfly's ball and the Grasshopper's feast."

Among the high-stepping, and kicking, fillies, Miss Pettigrew met was Edythe Dubarry, the young owner of a fashionable beauty parlor. When Miss Pettigrew's asked how she came to own the shop when she was a stripling, "Oh, that," Miss Dubarry replied. "That was very simple. I vamped the boss." On Miss Pettigrew's astonishment and wondering how she could "think of such a thing," Miss Dubarry repeated that it was simple, explaining that she had been an eighteen-year-old apprentice and "he was getting on." If you are clever, she continued, "they always fall for the young ones." "I was always clever that way," she elaborated. "If you act 'marriage or nothing,' they generally give you marriage. I was very lucky. I went to his head, but he couldn't stand the pace. He got a nice tombstone and I got the parlor." Such lessons are rarely taught in universities. "Or in churches," Vicki said; "what an oversight. When the snow melts, close your books and let's go to the 'Scarlet Peacock,' have a barnyard of cocktails, and applaud the chanteuse Delysia Lafosse, né Sarah Grub, Miss Pettigrew's great friend."

We did not visit the nightclub because December suddenly spread brighter than a peacock's tail. When I was young, my only ambition was to be a daddy, someone as decent and nice as my parents. "Rich man, poor man, beggar man," banker, lawyer—none of those mattered. For years since our children left home, Vicki and I have longed to be grandparents. In December Edward's wife Erica gave birth to Samuel Taylor Pickering, Taylor being one of Vicki's family names, and Samuel being the bud atop a long stem of Sammy's, not only me but my father, grandfather, great-great grandfather on and on into the seventeenth century, the list interrupted only twice, once for a Levi then for my great-grandfather William. Sammy's appearance was a surprise. A series of sad mishaps preceded his conception, and the chances of Edward and Erica's becoming parents seemed impossible. When Edward telephoned and announced Sammy's birth, Vicki and I were over the moon and stars with joy, laughing and crying simultaneously. At 79, I knew that I did not have time left to get to know the little boy. He and I would not spend the Children's Hour together. I wouldn't be around to ask him if the black sheep had any wool, and I'd never bounce him on a knee and hear him laugh when I told him about the cat and the fiddle and their vaulting barnyard companion, the cow who jumped over the moon. I would not tuck him in bed and put him to sleep singing "Sweet and Low" or William Bennett's "Lullaby! O, Lullaby! / Baby, hush that little cry! / Light is dying, / Bats are flying, / Bees to-day with work have done; / So, till comes the morrow's sun, / Let sleep kiss those bright eyes dry! / Lullaby! O Lullaby!"

But I was content. I was too happy to dry my emotions and hammer them into words. In hindsight, I seemed immersed in the mouldering stanzas of old newspaper and magazine verse—the kind of poetry that people once loved and recited, that made them weep and laugh before they hardened into sophistication. "Only a baby small," Matthias Barr wrote, "small, but how dear to us." I held Gerald Massey's "wee white rose of all the world." I heard poor Clare in her trundle bed ask, "Mamma, is there too many of we?" I saw little white hearses go "glimmering by," one carrying Little Joe who hoped there would be flowers in heaven, in another Baby who reassured her family saying, "Be better in the mornin'—bye." Although "A Stray Sunbeam" also led to a grave, it was happier. The father of a wayward boy fell in battle and left a widow "with this babe to fight her way through life." She worshipped her darling and living for him alone waited for the day when he would "be her strong protector through her declining years." Unfortunately, as the boy grew older, he forsook virtue and his mother. He drank and gambled and making her life a torture "broke her living heart." One night when "his brain was all afire," he received a message from a minister urging him to hurry home because his mother was dying.

He arrived home too late. Folded on her breast "were the patient, loving hands that oft had laid her boy to rest, / And the lips that kissed the clustering curls from off his boyhood's brow / Were pale, and cold, and lifeless." To no avail, he cried, "Come back, my mother." He fell to his knees beside her corpse and asking God to forgive his bad behavior, begged Him to "let my mother's spirit watch o'er her wayward son." His prayers were answered. He reformed and giving up liquor, became known for kindness and good deeds. One gloomy day after a year had passed since his mother's death, he visited her grave at twilight. As he stood beside her mound, he testified that her spirit had made him strong and brave and addressing her as "angel mother" begged her to guide him ever onward, until we meet again." Although the sun had set, "a little sunbeam, a little silvery ray" broke through the "darkling clouds" and lingered on his forehead "with a soft caressing air." "Deny not this," the poem concluded, "That little straying sunbeam was his angel mother's kiss." I won't read "A Stray Sunbeam" again. Months from now remembering it will make me queasy, and that's lamentable. Only occasionally will I think about the poetry of life, be it good or bad. But for now, Sammy, as Thomas Dekker put it, "Golden slumbers kiss your eyes, / Smiles awake you when you rise."

"Because my love is come to me," Christina Rossetti wrote in "A Birthday," "My heart is like a singing bird /whose nest is in a watered shoot; / My heart is like an apple tree / Whose boughs are bent with fruit." Because Sammy came to us, Vicki's and my feelings also sang. "Now," Vicki wrote Edward. "I have another little body to love and worry about and over, to include in my fervent 'prayers,' and to make a wish for on every full moon. I feel like my heart is a sponge all squeezed up tight with emotion." "This intensity is strange and seems more acute than I had in giving birth to my own children," she continued. "But you see, memory and time play tricks. I cannot remember what I felt or went through forty years ago. Also, the struggles and hurdles you have had to go through, we did not experience back then. And yet we have lived them and felt them very profoundly with you. It is a momentous thing—the miracle of birth." Vicki's and my experiences were very different from those of Erica and Edward. There was no ultrasound or barrage of tests. Erica's friends held a baby shower for her, and unlike our three children, Sammy had drawers of clothes decorated with a zoo of creatures: a white moose, orange giraffes, brown bears with bulging white tummies, and elephants with ears like wings. A red fox and his buddy a hedgehog scampered across a yard. Long-legged zebras and rainbow-colored dinosaurs with goofy tusks were eager to play with him. At night a blue blanket bright with a yellow moon and constellations of stars, all with kind smiley faces, covered and watched over him.

    Vicki and I had lived in Storrs less than two years when Francis was born, and we had few friends. The only item of baby clothes that I remember is a silk gown in which Vicki's father had been christened. Of course we had much more. Mother and Father came to Connecticut almost before Francis's birth, and they never travelled without a hamper of gifts. Memory always parses. It is a serviceable but weak vessel. Its holds are limited and capable of transporting only a fraction of one's experiences across the seas of time. Edward wrote us every day. He told us that he put a picture of Vicki and me on a bookshelf overlooking Sammy's crib. "Bookended," he said, by *Brown Bear, Brown Bear, What'd You See?* and *Saint George and the Dragon.* Erica tended to Sammy during the night. At four in the morning a "shift change" occurred and Edward took Sammy. "These morning hours with him during these early, early days are very special," Edward wrote. "I know they will fly by. We sit quietly in the dimly lit nursery until Erica gets up several hours later."

As I read Edward's correspondence, a crowd of lost memories emerged. Francis was born early one morning. Afterward I left the hospital and taught. Students know everything and nothing. Although I hadn't mentioned Vicki's and my expecting a baby, they knew, and when I walked into the classroom at eight that morning, they started cheering and shouting. They read my face and reacted to my happiness with warm delight. For me all the years of teaching resembled that day. They were rich and rewarding, humanizing. They were epiphanies that prevented the hard corns of cynicism from forming. As I remembered those children smiling and clapping, I thought about Father. He would have been a marvelous teacher. Once I asked him why he didn't go to graduate school. He explained that he came from a small country town and a small country school and entered college at sixteen. Because he had little money, he often held three jobs at once, He was popular and smart, but when judged by grades, he wasn't a candidate for graduate school. That, of course, is the marking fallacy. What matters are affection for people and a fondness for books. Many years later Walter asked a literary woman if she had read any of my volumes. "Sam, Jr.," she said. "didn't write those books. Big Sam did. He's the wittiest man in Nashville." "When your mama smiled," he once said to me, "everybody smiled back." "Looking at you three," I wrote Edward, holding in my hand a picture of him and Erica gazing at Sammy, "makes me think of Mommy and Daddy. How we loved each other!"

A video of Sammy's crying brought Edward's childhood to mind. He was the family's champion wailer. "I walked you upstairs and downstairs, night and day," I wrote him. "I was the walker and consoler, back patter and coo-er." I told him the video tightened my chest, making me want to walk Sammy as I did him "those decades ago." "I don't know what to make of life and time," I concluded. "What is true is that I put only fleeting moments on the page. It is also true that I decided not to write anything that would make you children wince when you were forty years old. That means I distorted life and, in effect, lied, something I continue to do. As an honorable man never believes more than a fifth of what he says, so decent autobiographical essayists always redact their pages. Perhaps I ought not to have done so."

Sixty years ago in the attic of my childhood home in Nashville, I discovered the love letters Father wrote Mother in the 1930s. Mother tied a pink ribbon around them and stored them in a steamer trunk along with the clothes of another generation: corsets, camisoles, and leather high-buttoned shoes. I didn't read the letters. After untying the ribbon and glancing at the letter on top, I retied the ribbon and buried the letters at the bottom of the trunk. Later when cleaning out the attic, I sent the old clothes to the dump and shredded the letters. "That was a mistake," Vicki said. "The letters told a story." "Yes," I answered, "a closeted domestic story—the progress of my parents' courtship, not for my eyes or those of strangers who read my books." "You'll regret not keeping the letters and writing about them," Vicki said. "I did the right thing," I replied. Propriety was an element of the air I breathed growing up in the 1940s. Often it inhibited and was repressive. Certainly, it stifled experimentation, but then in my household manners were extraordinarily important. They mattered more than laws. Manners calmed, supported civility, soothed and elevated, and were responsible for kindly common-sensical restraint. Today things have changed. Honesty is "too much with us." The confessional, my friend Josh says, has moved from the church to the television. Much of what was once kept private is now celebrated in public. "Poor form" doesn't apply to deportment but to athletic skills.

High spirits disturb. Days devoid of joy are easier than those with it, especially for older people who long for stability and calm of mind and emotions. Jubilation and fear accompanied the births of Vicki's and my children. Every night for years, I went into the children's rooms and put my index finger under their noses to see if they were breathing. As they became adults, the fear lessened but never completely vanished. Now Sammy's birth has intensified it. At night I don't walk across the upstairs landing into another bedroom, but I wake up worried. Sometimes my cheeks are wet. Although the worries themselves are vague, I know their source.

The Christmas letters I received described not only accounts of old lives ending, but also of young lives ruined. Because the latter descriptions were unbearable, I did not write about them. My silence distorted life, but living with truth is impossible. In October I read *As It Is In Heaven*. Written by Mark Sparkes Wheeler and published in 1906, the book describes an allegorical journey through heaven taken by "One of the Redeemed." As the narrator explores heaven, she experiences a series of didactic, inspirational encounters. In one she meets a man whose baby "went up to the warm sun" when only two years old. Although the man knows his child has gone to the "real world" where there is no death and it is always morning, he is grief-stricken and says his heart resembles the ground from which "a storm had torn a great tree." "I could begin the world again without a loaf or a friend if I had but thee," he says addressing his lost child. "O baby! Sweet, sweet baby!" he says tearfully. "1 will try for your sake to be a better man; I will be kind to other little babies, and tell them your name, and sometimes let them play with your toys; but, oh, baby! baby! My old heart throbs and breaks."

Vicki once accused me of reading "every terrible book" written during the Romantic and Victorian Ages. If I'd read fewer books, maybe life would be more placid and I wouldn't fret about Sammy. The moods of the elderly are recurrent, but fortunately like their attention spans are short-lived. The gloom of today probably won't be the gloom of tomorrow. But it may be the gloom of the day after tomorrow. I did not linger in Heaven with the Redeemed. Instead I pondered Fate. It is, I think, another name for inheritance, not financial but physical and mental, a person's susceptibility to certain diseases, for example, among males in my family, thyroid and prostate ailments. In contrast we seem immune to dementia, and only when air forsakes us, do we cease pronouncing. We are not ambitious and discourage attention. However, we are given to quoting. Referring to people who covet acclaim and fawn over celebrity, Alexander Smith said, "A gentleman gains nothing by covering his fingers with rings." The political currents that swirl through days dampen out spirits and occasionally cause us to gag, but they don't loosen our grips on sense. Addictions don't undermine us, and we have a propensity to be lucky, in contrast to most people for whom luck is random and arbitrary, indeed is luck. We may not look like one another, but we behave similarly. Of course it is flattering to see one's self in his offspring. Eliza inherited my impatience "with fools," and Francis the absence of calves on his legs.

When I was a young, Father read to me. Uncle Wiggily Longears took me for rides in his automobile. If he were hungry, he gobbled down his turnip steering wheel, and our trips were short. After dinner Uncle Remus let me sit on his knee. He stroked my head and told me about the antics of Brer Rabbit and Brer Fox. One night he gave me a genuine Pimmerly Plum, dipped in sugar and a present from Brer Tarrypin for "the little boy." I began reading to the children soon after their births. I read at least an hour a day for eight or nine years. I stopped only when the busy work of school assignments started demanding large hunks of their bedtime. Like Father and me before him, Edward is reading to Sammy—board books and picture books, fables and fairy tales, anything, even though Sammy is only a month old. As a genealogist familiar with my writing would predict, Edward also reads poetry. How can a father resist the charms of Mother Hubbard and her pipe-smoking, flute playing mongrel, and of watching the mouse run up and down the clock at one in the evening, his three blind cousins huddled at the bracket feet remembering the gay time before their tails were docked and they scampered from shelf to shelf in the pantry? How marvelous to listen to duet of Little Boy Blue blowing his horn and the bells of St. Clement's saying "oranges and lemons."

Reading will surely turn Edward and Sammy into good Samaritans. They'll cheer up Wednesday's child, stop Georgie Porgie from kissing girls and making them cry, and save Tommy Stout from the difficult and dangerous task of extracting pussy from the well. Their beneficence will make them feel so good about themselves that they might come to like Dr. Fell. Reading will educate their confidence, and maybe they can prevent the man in the moon from coming down too soon and burning his mouth with cold plum porridge. Of course strenuous reading increases the appetite, but Polly can put the kettle on, and father and son share a bowl of pease porridge hot. If a limb falls onto power lines and knocks the electricity out, and if they don't have a generator as Vicki and I do, they can call Jeremiah. He'd lay a fire and blow the flames puff, puff, puff.

Edward is a higher cultural flyer that I. Last week he read Coleridge's poetry to Sammy. When I read, Edward wrote, "Sammy shapes his mouth into a little 'o' and opening his eyes wide, raises his eyebrows and gazes to the right and the left. He resembles a painted cherub captured in the very instant of being surprised by something from on high." The poem that delighted Edward the most and likely Sammy, too, was "Frost at Midnight." The poem is meditative. Coleridge's home is silent, and the members of his household are in bed. As Edward sits by himself in South Carolina early in the morning holding his sleeping son, so at midnight in the Lake District Coleridge is alone except for his son, "my cradled infant," slumbering beside him. Coleridge stares into the "low burnt" fire, and addressing the boy ponders the years that will stretch ahead. "My babe so beautiful! It thrills my heart / With tender gladness, thus to look at thee, / And think that thou shalt learn far other lore, / And far other scenes!" He recalls that he was reared in a great city whereas his son "shalt wander like breeze / By lakes and sandy shores, beneath the crags / Of ancient mountains." In these surroundings the Universal Teacher whose presence is manifested in Nature shall, he writes, "mold thy spirit." I taught "Frost at Midnight" for years. Not until Edward described reading it to his cradled infant did the poem seem other than thoughts nicely phrased. Now its words play across my feelings like fingers plucking the strings of a lyre. I, too, hope all seasons shall be sweet to my thee—greening spring, lusty summer, auburn fall, and tufted, blowing winter.

 January is here. Advent and Christmas are over, and the next solstice is six months away. I have plenty of time to answer my December letters. I'll anticipate the June solstice by keeping on the sunny side unless the day is sweltering. In that case I might dip into the shade and rest for a paragraph or two. Thirty-five years ago I planted a Chinese witch hazel in the dell outside my study. In November it resembled a parade of yellow confetti. Then in early December a wind storm felled a black birch, dropping it on and shattering the witch hazel, reducing its trunk to a low splintered stob. In May Vicki and I will drive to Logee's greenhouse in Danielson in hopes of finding a replacement. We need something hardy. Green doesn't last in the yard, or, alas, in life. To paraphrase Thomas Nashe: flowers are beauties that Time devours. Once the dell was a slope of daffodils, but run-off from the chemicals sprayed on the road in front of the house to melt snow and ice poisoned them. Maybe atop a slope above the runoff we'll plant a redbud —no, two redbuds—-or perhaps a couple of shadbushes, trees that will shine like stray sunbeams despite "darkling clouds."

 I'm not sure what books I will read. Unlike the

conclusions envisioned in their letters by most of my December correspondents, the books will have happy, open-ended, promising endings—frog-princes, marriages, Champagne, talking cats, and beasts transformed into beauties. I'll only drift from such tales if I stumble across novels that have eluded me for years, particularly, *Zelma Yegg, The Beautiful Maniac* and *Mr. Moto and the Cyclops with the Glass Eye*. This kind of reading diverts and helps old men avoid devolving into dismissive curmudgeons plagued by fret and misgiving. Like straight roads that point relentlessly toward barren horizons, sometimes lives top unforeseen rises and suddenly descend into dips curvy and lush and green. In any case, I won't deaden the pleasures of reading and subject books to the forceps and retractors of criticism. "A knowledge of books ought to give a man a delicate allusiveness, an aptitude for pointed quotation," A. C. Benson wrote. "A book ought to be only incidentally, not anatomically, discussed." Throughout spring and summer, I'll study woods and fields and write prose because details of budding and blooming will be obvious. Poetry suits winter better than prose because when a person is snow bound his imagination sees more than do his eyes. Details don't fence in the fanciful. Maybe in September, Vicki and I will make a birthday pilgrimage to the tomb of the Unknown Pacifist. Next to the monument is a stone on which is engraved Miller Williams's poem "Compassion." "Have compassion for everyone you meet / even if they don't want it. What seems conceit, / even bad manners, or cynicism is always a sign / of things no ears have heard, no eyes have seen. / You do not know what wars are going on / down there where the spirit meets the bone."

Few people, so far not I, can live up to Williams'

urging. Still, my birthday is nine months away. Who knows what changes tomorrow will bring? Well, actually I do know. Tomorrow a deep snow is supposed to fall and that's all right; Afterward Vicki and I will follow Elinor Wylie's lyrical suggestion in "Velvet Shoes."

> Let us walk in the white snow
> In a soundless space;
> With footsteps quiet and slow,
> At a tranquil pace,
> Under veils of white lace.
>
> I shall go shod in silk,
> And you in wool,
> White as a white cow's milk,
> More beautiful
> Than the breast of a gull.

Notes

"When found, make a note of," Captain Cuttle advises Walter Gay in *Dombey and Son*. In Jill McCorkle's novel *Hieroglyphics* Lil one of the main characters is aging into losing both her past and the present. To prevent her life from slipping into the chaos of the forgotten and the misremembered, she writes notes to herself and leaves them throughout her house. As people themselves become footnotes, so their lives and the worlds they inhabit eventually become composed of notes, not of days and years, not the light that shined from Adam's body, not blood and bone, earth and sky, but simply notes.

  Vicki's and my kitchen is a pinched 1940s room, measuring eighteen by fifteen feet. There is no island, little counter space, and no place to sit. What there is a forest of notes. Attached to the fronts of the cabinets are seventy-two notes, most pale yellow, three-inch square Post-its, the writing on them in pencil: "Call Barbara," "Sam—Dr. Chen—Wednesday—June 23rd—9:00," "Garden Barn Vernon," "Don't Leave Napkins on the Chair," "Eat Slowly-NO Snacking," and "Vicki Don't Click On Any Links." A few notes are mathematical, for example, marks in groups of five tallying the number of mice trapped in the basement the past two winters, at the moment 94. One note reckons the number of corks in a box. On each level of the box are 84 corks. The box has 9 layers with one cork free-floating for a total of 757 corks. Some notes are mystifying, their subjects forgotten. Only one is sinister "Conservation Burial," and it is glued to a wall beside a sign depicting a gray squirrel and reading "Welcome to the Nut House."

Notes paper the door and one side of the refrigerator. They burst out in clusters like the palmate leaves on horse chestnut trees, the leaflets not joined at a stem but held together by magnets. Among the magnets are an aviary of birds: a bluebird, a robin, a chickadee, a white leghorn chicken nesting in a round Nantucket basket, an olive warbler, three hummingbirds, and a pair of metal flamingoes purchased in and flown home from the Caribbean. Three beetles also crawl across the door. Identifying beetles is difficult, especially as these have fed on vegetable steroids and measure two and a half inches long, an inch and a quarter broad, and when upright and scurrying an inch and a half tall. Their body shapes are oval and their elytra are colorful, green pleated with black stripes, orange and black, then black with a red cumber bun, these last two speckled with green. Their artistic illegitimacy obscures their origins, but they appear sports of Colorado Potato and Ladybug beetles.

The refrigerator attracts and without rancor hosts a diversity of magnets: a seahorse, two ceramic wooden shoes, a Turk's Head cactus from Turks and Caicos, a blue tang from Bonaire, a view from the walls above the dry moat of Castillo San Felipe Del Morro Citadel in San Juan, flags of Connecticut and Dominica, and a pack of rescue dogs all toothy and grinning like movie stars. The magnets themselves reveal interests, map travels and in effect are notes. On the door of the spice cabinet is a mosaic composed of another species of note, fourteen postcards sent by our son Francis from Tasmania, Scotland, Austria, Germany, British Columbia, and then closer to home Maine and Vermont, places in which he has mountain biked. Stored in a drawer of a 1790s English chest in what once a formal dining room are two stacks of other postcards. Initially rubber bands bound the cards. But the rubber rotted, and the bands broke, and now string ties the cards together.

    Calendars are flat sheets of notes. In the kitchen there are three; in my study two, all having been sent by environment organizations like Audubon and The Nature Conservancy as thanks for donations. On this month's pages on the two calendars in the study appear a bobolink perched on scrub in hayfield and a female rufous hummingbird hovering over a cornucopia of blue blossoms. Often what purports to simplify leads to complexity. Instead of helping to remember, the calendars confuse. What is written on one calendar never makes it to all five, and sometimes appointments scheduled carefully are missed. Making matters worse is that twelve times a year the face page of each calendar must be flipped over to the next month. Inevitably some pages are neglected and don't get turned with the result that people with foggy vision don't notice that they're looking at March when the month is actually April, or more than likely May or June.

    Occasionally I determine to shake free from the tightening Procrustean bed of notes. I always fail. Last month I threw away a thirty-eight and three-quarter inch stack of lined five-by-eight-inch note cards. Both sides of almost all the cards were covered with excerpts coped in No. 2 pencils from 18th and 17th century books and journals. The cards were the result of years of research and living—gleanings from the British Museum, Welcome Institute, and Dr Williams's Library, among quadrangles of others. From them I wrote three academic books and some thirty articles. Glancing at the stack frightened me. I didn't want to dive back into the cards and begin another book. Even worse, studying them would make me remember the past. I'd regret opportunities missed and lament happiness impossible to relive. Rereading them would upset the soporific but safe tenor of the present, and I'd fret about the whys of actualities and those of the imagination.

Throwing away all that paper life was difficult, so I compromised. I behaved like a Protestant scripture dowser opening the bible at random in hopes of discovering the water of life "bright as crystal." From each handful of cards I dropped into the recycle bin, I arbitrarily removed one. None directed me to "the throne of God and of the Lamb." But a couple were moral. In *Choice Emblems, Natural, Historical, Fabulous, Moral, and Divine* published in 1790, John Huddlestone Wynne warned "Of the Danger of Greatness." If a person "wouldst taste the serene joys of life, fly far from greatness," Wynne advised, "and make thy abode with the daughter of simplicity." In *The Christian Mirror* (1805), A.B. described the "Excellencies" of Christianity. "In every worldly path, my feet were pierced with thorns, clouds of darkness were before my eyes wherever I turned them, whatever I grasped it broke like a bubble in my hand," A. B. testified. "God, dwelling in Christ, appeared to be the only ark where my feet could rest—the only sun that could enlighten my darkness—the only satisfying portion in whom, through all the vicissitudes of life, and at the gloomy hour of death, I might rejoice." Thomas Paine's bible differed greatly from A.B.'s New Testament. "There are matters in that book, said to be done by *the express command* of God," Paine wrote, "that are as shocking to humanity, and to every idea we have of moral justice, as anything done by Robespierre, by Carrier, Joseph Le Bon, in France; by the English government, in the East Indies."

I don't believe that religion or education can reform humanity. As a result I prefer my morality light and unpretentious like a poem in *Jacky Dandy's Delight* published in Edinburgh in 1815. "The little good boy, / That will not tell a lie, / Shall have a Plumb-pudding, / Or hot Apple pye; / But he that is naughty, / And tells a false tale, / Shall have nothing else / But a whip to his tail." In the ten or so cards I chanced upon, boys were not popular. In Dorothy Kilner's *The Rational Brutes; or, Talking Animals* (1799), an Ass said, "I think it would be the happiest thing for this nation that was ever yet thought of, if some plan could be contrived to destroy every *boy* upon the island. There is certainly no animal in the creation so destructive as *boys*; they do more mischief than all the race of *foxes*, *rats*, or *hedgehogs* put together, and are ten times more barbarous than hornets or gadflies. If it was not for boys, one might pass one's time comfortably enough; but they destroy the happiness of one's life by their inhumanity, and their tricks." For the record, girls did not pass uncriticized through the pages of early children's books. But no account of female misbehavior surfaced when I was dowsing, obliquely mirroring, Josh said, "the contemporary doings of university Star Chambers." Josh suffers inordinately from the colic. Perhaps, if he followed the suggestion made by John Banester in the seventeenth century and swallowed a beaker bubbling with the "oyle of ivie," the verminous matter would be expelled. Afterward his speech would probably be temperate and not windy or distempered.

What appeared on many of the cards I removed from the stack were medical matters. On her deathbed Florence Kidder gazed upward and said, "I am going—I am going—Come Lord Jesus, come quickly—O Lord, receive me." Florence was eleven years old and suffered from tuberculosis and religious melancholia. Thomas Paine could have cured the latter, and perhaps a different treatment might have alleviated the former. In the 17th century Thomas Bright urged the British to change the drugs they took. I don't see why, he wrote, "the medicines of India, or Aegypt should be laide upon us, more than the Indian or Aegyptian diet, which is to eate Lizards, Dragons, and Crocodiles: for if the proper medicine doth always regard his proper adversarie, which causeth the disease (as no doubt it should doe) then there being a great difference betwixt our humours and theirs, as much in a manner as is betwixt the flesh of a Crocodile and of a tender Capon, our medicines which are to fit us must needs be of another kinde than theirs." Perhaps a new prescription would have helped poor Florence, maybe a return to cure-alls imported from the Levant, although mummy dust or mummia had been discredited by the time of her death early in the 19th century.

Escaping medical notes is impossible for people my age. Every morning I take five or so pills, the names of which I cannot spell or pronounce. Moreover I have no idea what their effects are and often think eating lizards' tails and washing tablespoons of mummy dust down my gullet would benefit me more. With the exception of days on which the dogs are scheduled to receive heartworm pills, almost all the markings on the five calendars are reminders of doctors' appointments. At each appointment an assistant greets me carrying a sheaf of notes. The notes are in effect my identity. I am the pills I take, the operations and sicknesses I've had, and the ailments which plague me. I had my tonsils removed when I was three or four. My little finger was broken in a high school football game and operated on twenty-six years later, and I ripped a meniscus while racing downhill in my fifties, the two injuries illustrating that sports are harmful to one's health. Twice my collar bones have been broken, once in kindergarten when four proper little girls piled atop me in a game of ring around the rosy. Five years ago I crashed my bicycle and broke my left arm. I am a safer driver than bicyclist, and I have never been given a ticket or bumped or been bumped by another motorist.

A carcinoma has been dug out of my colon and another sliced out of my neck. For nine years I've had atrial fibrillations. Thrice doctors stopped and restarted my heart in hopes of shocking the beat into a sensible rhythm. Their efforts failed, and there will not be a fourth attempt, not even one managed by Dr. Asclepius at Massachusetts General Hospital. My wisdom teeth have been pulled and cataracts removed from both eyes. I've lost one parathyroid and half my thyroid. Three decades ago the day before a neck operation I checked myself out of a hospital because I worried that the surgeon might slip and leave my three small children with a ga-ga father. Never have I visited a nerve mechanic in his repair shop, and the only consultants to whom I've talked consulted me, not I, them. I've had chicken pox and both red and German measles. I have never had the mumps or whooping cough, and during bad polio years spent summers quarantined in deep country. I don't smoke and haven't sampled recreational drugs. However, a pharmaceutical that I've never considered trying now reduces anxiety and helps calm my hours. Our dog Suzie is sixteen years old, deaf, almost blind, and has slipped the collar of canine reason. At three in the afternoon she starts racing from room to room, chortling incessantly, getting underfoot, and tripping me trying to cadge food. She doesn't stop after her dinner but continues reinvigorated, or at least did so until recently. Vicki and I have copied sensible soap opera nurses and to preserve our well-being now keep our unruly patient doped "to the gills." Every night at dinner, Vicki inserts half a gram of melatonin into a nibble of liverwurst and feeds it to Suzie. Thirty minutes later Suzie is conked out, and at nine o'clock when I carry her outside, she barely wakes. "A Mickey Finn for the four-legged," Vicki says. Vicki and I are enablers. We have watched a lot of television shows about addicts, and we know if the half gram loses its kick, to increase the dose.

For four decades I haven't drunk spirits although if Vicki serves a spicy dish at dinner, I might drink a beer. Early in February, the coronavirus nailed me, and knocked out my taster and sniffer for six months. Lastly when a physician's assistant asks impertinent lame-brained questions about my mental health, I respond poorly. The first question is usually, "Do you ever feel depressed?" The person who says he is never depressed is either a liar, an imbecile, or is mentally ill. In fact depression is a sign of intelligence. The smarter a person the more often he gets depressed. The deeper the thinker the darker the melancholy. The better a person behaves the more splenetic his moods. Who does not moan when he compares what is with what could or should be? Only the senile are optimistic at eighty. I'm not rude, but I quickly derail inquisitors asking if he, or, more than likely, she has a pet. They always do.

    At doctors' appointments the sheets are me. No matter how many cards one throws away, he cannot escape medical notations. Moreover, time rarely changes all a person's behavior. I tally things other than mice. Frequently I try to stop. Sometimes I succeed. One night in March after waking up at 2:22, I put a notecard and pencil on my bedside table. I then began keeping track of the nights when I was awake at 2:22. After recording twenty-two nights, I stopped and recycled the card. I do not know whether repetition disturbs or reassures me. I threw a box containing medals given to participants in road races into the recycle bin along with the research notes. Years ago I jettisoned the few trophies I won. The writing on cards devoted to my sporting life is in soft pencil and has faded into the abstract. Only a duplicitous autobiographer could decipher the words. I was a hapless but intelligent athlete, that is, I had no talents but was smart enough to play only for fun. To emend Grantland Rice, when the one great scorer comes to mark against my name, it will be obvious that I didn't give a hoot whether I won or lost. Nine years ago shortly after I retired, I threw away 716 long yellow pages of lectures on environmental writers. I had worked on them for over twenty years. The lines on the pages were single-spaced. The font was small, and the pages thick with learning. In them lay the chapters of a thoughtful book on nature writers. I rid myself of the lectures because I did not want to write the book. I wanted to mull my thoughts and my observations rather than analyzing those of others.

I didn't want to be recognized as a critic of nature writing, indeed of anything specific. I preferred to observe birds and insects and meander free from limiting taxonomy.

The notecards were stored in the attic. They were heavy and had to be loaded into boxes. Because Vicki thought I might fall and force her to schedule another doctor's appointment, she carried the cards downstairs, taking three trips to transport them to the study. Initially finding the cards was difficult. Eventually we discovered them beneath an ancient trundle bed behind breastworks of trunks and chairs. On the way we unearthed forty years of pay stubs, bank statements, and tax forms. In spring the Town of Mansfield sponsored "Shredding Day," so I sent the "book keeping" to the shredder, including copies of our most recent tax filings. No notecard describes me as an anarchist or libertarian. I've never attempted to finagle out of taxes. Indeed I usually pay before they are due, and probably pay more than I am liable for. But ridding the house of all those pages of notes and figures pumped me full of high spirits, almost as if I had purged rats from the world—ship, Norway, political, and social.

Attics and basements are the repositories of lives—storehouses of portraits and paintings, China, rugs, suitcases bulging with scrapbooks and memories, blanket chests, dressers, Hitchcock chairs, toy soldiers, picture albums, armoires of clothes, and in my case, Civil War memorabilia: newspapers, songbooks, wills, and innumerable letters. Such things are notes that mark passing. People are collectors and ultimately the collectibles become them, notes gathered during their lives and left behind after their deaths. The figurines on the living room mantlepiece are, in a sense, notes describing my days. The books in the study reveal as much about me as do my medical records. Possessions attract anecdotes which in turn become not simply the tales of a life but the life itself. Bodies disappear, but stories endure. My friend Mike was an acclaimed historian, but whenever old friends reminisced about him, they described the time he returned home fuddled and thinking his closet the lavatory urinated on his shoes. Henry was a mathematician. Sometime during his career he solved an unsolvable problem. However his graduate school companions remember him as a poet. One evening at dinner, Henry said he'd spent the afternoon writing a poem in the parking lot near the Graduate College at Princeton. He monopolized dinner conversation explaining the importance of matters such as meter and caesura in the course of which he mentioned devices like anaphora, metonymy, and chiasmus, simultaneously boring and mystifying everyone at the table. Eventually he said that he'd only managed to write the last line of the poem, noting, however, that the meter was perfect. After pausing to see that people around the table were awake, he recited the line, "And that's the way you change a tire." On another occasion he meticulously described the similarities between the verse of Wordsworth and Coleridge and his new poem "Solitude." "I was all alone. / I was by myself. / There was no one with me."

  Only if our children sift carefully through the house reading the unwritten notes stored here and there will they know Vicki and me. Even then the chore will be impossibly onerous and after removing the notes which can be easily monetized, they should and will toss the rest into the recycle barrel. To imply that everything kept, recorded or shaped is a note so expands the definition of the word that it would seem to lose meaning. But it doesn't. As the worn notecards disclose much about my past, so the notes in the kitchen reveal much about the present. All people are note takers and makers. Writers mark pages. Gardeners mark the ground, and travelers buy souvenirs. A person doesn't always have to find things before making a note. Often notes come ready-made. Recently a former student wrote me. Because of the coronavirus he'd spent the past year working at home. As a result he had more "family time." On most days, he recounted, "I play tag with my little girls for hours, and I think I'm getting pretty good at it, but I never win." "Good for you," I replied, noting, "I played games with my children for years, and they always beat me. Because I lost, I won."

My listening to music at night keeps Vicki from falling to sleep. It has so provoked her that she composed the libretto for "The Tablecloth," an opera both domestic and exotic, she says. "Oh, woe is me, red wine spilled all over the tablecloth," a soprano and wife begins. "Oh, it matters not. I'll buy you a dozen more," the husband "a tenor or baritone or possible base" responds. "But, no!," the wife exclaims. "It is a piece of your mother's heirloom linen. She will think I am an unfit wife! Oh, I am doomed! She comes!" "Fear not!," the husband suggests, "Lock her in the closet!" "How can I?" the wife asks, "I must distract her somehow!" "Oh, woe is me, how I have suffered my mother's harsh words and at her hands my whole life," sings the husband. "Be a man. Stand up to her!" the wife urges. The husband, alas, is a spendthrift and is too poor to purchase a replacement tablecloth. The couple are barely getting by on a "dwindling income." Moreover they live on an estate (probably

Russian) far from a specialist cleaner and on which the peasants refuse to work because they have not been paid in months. The opera will need polishing before it is staged at La Scala, but it is good enough for the Pickering House. I put it in a satchel and stored it in the attic. When the children find it years from now, they will make a note of it. But now to adapt Wynne's remarks in *Choice Emblems* to the present, I am preparing to fly from writing and enjoy one of the serene joys of life, rereading *Dombey and Son*. "Heart's Delight," as Captain Cuttle was fond of saying, a phrase I found and made a note of in the 1970s when I was writing about Dickens.

Endings

"The world is so full of a number of things that no man with a grain of poetry or the scientific spirit in him has any right to be bored," Robert Lynd wrote. Weariness, not boredom, affects the lives of the elderly. Years of being kind, compassionate, and responsible tire a person. How long does a person have the strength and inclination to appear smart or charming? "He should have been a snake charmer," Josh said describing a witty acquaintance. "In his presence King Cobras slithered off their thrones, dropped their fangs, smiled, and purred. But what an effort it took to go through life as a social fakir playing the pungi every day. Imagine the tedium. If it didn't destroy the soul, it would wreck the hearing." "As for you," Josh said addressing me. "For years you've written before sunrise. Aren't you exhausted?"

Some days I can't muster the strength to pick up a pencil. Words are light. My pages don't weigh much, and writing shouldn't tire me. Sometimes I blame age, other times, the malingering effects of my tussle with the coronavirus. Probably the actual cause is last fall's treatment for cancer. It sapped my energy and eradicated the scribbling me whom I knew well and greeted every morning. "Just for a couple more years of life, I lost me," I told Josh. The person who took his place is okay. He is politer and certainly not so bawdy, but he is a stranger, and strangers lose their attraction as a person ages. "I know what I just wrote sounds silly," I thought. "But it isn't." Certainly, as people age, they divest themselves of habits, desires, property, and worries. Most lighten their lives without the aid of radiation. "We sold our boat which we had in Port Grimaud, near St. Tropez, two years ago and the apartment in 2019," Herbie, a rowing companion from my years St. Cat's, wrote this spring. "The appearance of the virus turned that into a very wise decision as we would have had all the costs and none of enjoyment. It had run its course anyway and we still have many happy memories of the times we spent there and absolutely no regrets."

Most divestments are not financial but unconscious as names and words suddenly vanish. Josh says he experiences the sense of a pipe's being plugged somewhere between his mind and his tongue. Happily, the unexpected arrives and like a rotorooter snakes though the hippocampus and grinds away some of the gunk. In January, the daughter of a former student of mine at Montgomery Bell Academy in Nashville wrote me. For years her father had been in business, but in middle age he changed his life and became a high school English teacher. He was now retiring from teaching, and she asked me to write him congratulatory letter. "He loved your class and talked about it often when I was in elementary school and he was working on a graduate degree in education." The man was a student in a sophomore English class I taught in 1966, fifty-five years ago. He was sixteen, and I was twenty-four. Now he was seventy-one and I, almost eighty.

Remembering my former student, now senior citizen, brought the year I taught at MBA to mind: my classroom half hidden by an oak, my "Spreading Chestnut Tree," the writers I taught, among them

Stephen Crane and Walt Whitman, afternoons spent coaching, having fun but not caring if teams won or lost, and the smooth optimistic faces of the boys, more than a few of whom are now dead, others brow-rumpled men whom I'd not recognize if I saw them. As having a good memory isn't necessarily good, so having a poor memory isn't necessarily bad. It frees one from the prison house of truth, to bring Wordsworth to mind. It allows a person to fabricate times that never existed "when meadow, grove, and stream" and "every common sight" seemed appareled, not in "celestial light," but simply in light. For the older writer, pondering gone years often leads to a wistful celebration of the past at the expense of the present. In the early nineteenth century the South African poet Thomas Pringle began "Afar in the Desert" lyrically writing, "Afar in the Desert I love to ride, / With the silent Bush-boy by my side: / When the sorrows of life the soul o'ercast, / And, sick of the Present, I cling to the Past." In this ending, I pack the past away. Of course as I have implied repeatedly, simple things aren't always simple. At a time when Vicki says that I ooze "attar of the invalid," I might follow Pringle and momentarily indulge in fond recollections, many of which will be partly true.

In *The Old Virginia Gentleman*, George Bagby declared that he had "a passion for porches." Quoting Keats, he said a porch was "a thing of beauty—a joy forever" except in very cold weather. "If I had the building of a house," he testified, "I would make it mostly of porches, upper and lower, with a room or so hung here and there on a nail driven into pillars." Vicki and I are porch less. Our home is modest, built in the early 1940s as a faculty house. One step leads down from the garage into the back yard, but it too narrow to sit on, and if we were able to do so, our legs would cramp. There is a stoop by the front door, but it is too small to accommodate chairs. If I had my druthers, porches would wrap the house. However, they wouldn't lurk in the shadows of columns and history as porches do in unlivable Southern ante-bellum mansions. At the imaginative minimum, my house would have twelve porches, one for every month of the year, those for the winter months closed in and heated. The lack of actual porches is not so much an absence as it is an opportunity. Because I'll spend less time at my desk, I'll be freer. I will roam the outdoors. The here's and the over-there's will be my porches. I'll furnish them with tree trunks, granite boulders, and high clay banks, appointments chosen for Vicki and me to sit on or lean against. I'll upholster them with moss and lichens. My taste like that of Mother is old-fashioned. In the spring I will cover them with Chintz: blossoms plucked from columbine, twinleaf, and Indian strawberry, speedwell, and ragged robin, these and more, all free at fancy's store. Nestled amid the flowers will be an assortment of toads, salamanders, shiny ground beetles, and I hope necklaces of green snakes. If we don't' rumple the covers, perhaps a hermit thrush will join us.

 Vicki and I will study the natural world and like Antaeus keep our feet on the ground both in mind and deed. Antaeus is the patron of environmentalists. His strength came from the earth. He was a great wrestler and was unbeatable provided he didn't lose contact with the ground—something most societies have done. Hercules knocked Antaeus off his feet and killed him. Today Hercules's progeny are earthmovers, bull dozers, trenchers, excavators, and monster trucks mythic in size. The places that nourished people and which strengthened their hard wood enabling them to be soft and knowing often vanish overnight. The dislocations so weaken people that they reflexively repeat the litanies prepared for them by secular theologians, celebrating the industrial gospels of progress and change.

I have always behaved almost rationally. Last week I dreamed I was falling asleep while driving. To prevent a crash, I woke myself and pulling onto a shoulder of the bed turned off the car's motor. Afterward I switched on the bedside light and read for half an hour, going to sleep safely at the book, not at the wheel. Next I dreamed I was reading a field guide to mushrooms. The going was tough. The book wasn't illustrated, and the language was technical and mysterious. Still, it kept me off the highway until the dogs began scratching at the kitchen door asking to be let out. I worry slightly that my porch conversations may be too common-sensical and resemble sermons. "Will a placid rocking-chair and pulpit life satisfy you?" Vicki asked pointedly. Vicki is often dubious of my intentions, not because I am weak-willed but because she thinks I'm "easily distracted." Hilaire Belloc once described an aged Sultan who counted the days in his long existence during which he had been content. The number was seventeen. If I become fretful and porch-crazy, I am sure the Great First Cause will intervene. He and most of his transcendent manifestations have reputations for benevolence. Surely, He or living itself will bring something to my attention that will force me off the porch and back to the desk for a short time. Yesterday the telephone in the television room was ringing when I walked into the house after jogging three miles. The print on the screen was too small for my eyes, so I answered the call. The First Cause had "blessed" me and delivered a wrong number. "Hello," I said. "Uh, this isn't Self-Expressions, is it?" a deep male voice asked. All my life I've been a barbershop, crew-cut guy. I think Self-Expressions is a gender-inclusive salon, specializing in taming unruly keratin and training it to the halter of curling iron and fashion. "Not exactly," I answered, "but if you feel compelled to self-express, let me make a suggestion." "Huh?" the man replied. He didn't say more because I forged ahead with my advice. "Go smack a Republican in the snoot." "What!" the man exclaimed, "I'm a Republican." "Good, that makes it easy," I continued, adding, "Are you at home?" On the man's saying "yes." I instructed him to go into his bedroom and stand in front of a mirror. "Study your image. Adjust your sights. Focus on your nostrils, and aim a fist at your nose. If your eyesight is good, then wham and you will have self-expressed." "What the," the man began. Because I find telephone profanity distasteful, I replaced the receiver in the cradle before the man finished talking.

"What was that call about?" Vicki asked. "Life, buzzing human-insect life," I answered. "A critic writing about old movies wanted to know what movies I watched as a child." "What did you tell him?" Vicki said. "I told him about Hopalong Cassidy and his great white horse Topper. Did you know that Topper is buried in a pet cemetery in Los Angeles?" "No," Vicki said. "Well you do now," I replied then asked who had come to the kitchen door while I was on the telephone. "Two anti-vaxxers, both women," Vicki said. When Vicki informed them that she'd been vaccinated, one of the women stated that Vicki erred. "The virus doesn't exist. I have not had a shot and never will," she said stridently. "Everything is in

God's hands, and He has already decided when I will die." "So that means if I get the ax out of the garage and chop off your head before you can run down the driveway, I won't be guilty of murder. God will. Your time was up. He turned me into Jehu and put the ax in my hands. How long do you suppose He will spend in jail for forcing me to send two presumptuous fools to Glory?" "What did the women say?" I asked. "They didn't say anything. They skedaddled." "They showed surprising sense," I said. Afterward I brewed a pot of Irish Breakfast Tea and going outside onto one of my unbuilt porches turned on a space heater and sat in an easy chair, feeling self-expressed and immensely cheered.

Unfortunately, I checked my email. The first mote that swam into sight was a university's "Gift Legacy eNewsletter." Sections of the letter focused on Finances, Personal Planning, and "Savvy Living." The initial article in this third section was "How to Choose a Quality Nursing Home During a Pandemic." "Can you give me some tips on how to pick a good nursing home in the Covid era?" the article began. "My mother had a stroke a while back and needs some extra care now. I have been taking care of her at home, but now I am unable to do it any longer." "Mother!" Vicki exclaimed. "Transparent as a Baby Doll nightie! The school's fund raisers assume that if the virus didn't knock the pins from under elderly alumni, it infected them with Burking Mania and made them aware of Old Man Mose, bony and peeled and riding a pale mule. Obviously, the fundsters think both the toothless and those long in the molars should write checks to the school while selecting harps and considering nursing homes for husbands, wives, or themselves. Dear old Mother was potted decades ago."

The mailbox is attached to the house beside the door to the porch. Shortly after escaping my inbox, I settled back into the predeath world and was sipping a second cup of tea when the mail arrived. Among a bill from Kohls, a warning that the warrantee on my car had expired, and a packet of "Heartgard Plus Chew Tabs" for Suzie the dog were a note from Edward and "The Bristol Years," the first chapter of a friend's autobiography. Edward wrote that when Sammy was "nestled or, rather, sunk, in his car seat, his chubby face collapsing on itself and pushing out his throat to create a second chin, his eyes slit as he hovers on the edge of sleep, that I picture his tongue darting out to an extraordinary length and nabbing a juicy fly." "Edward is our Antaeus, his eyes focused on groundlings," Vicki said. "Who else would spot Kenneth Grahame's Toad of Toad Hall, the terror, the traffic-queller, the Lord of the lone trail out for a jaunt in a motor-car?" Accompanying Edward's letter was a photograph of Sammy sitting in front of a chalk board. On the board Edward had written lines from Wordsworth's "Ode" celebrating the arrival of spring.

> The winds come to me from the fields of sleep,
> And all the earth is gay;
> Land and sea
> Give themselves up to jollity,
> And with the heart of May
> Doth every beast keep holiday;
> Thou Child of Joy.
> Shout round me, let me hear thy shouts, thou
>   happy Shepherd-boy!

"Wordsworth and poetry. Edward is your son and your father's grandson," Vicki said. "The old order doesn't yield to the new. It becomes the new." "I don't know if you're right, but the thought is nice and pleases me. I feel content," I said—and "uncomfortable" which I did not say. My feelings are simple and muted. Rarely do I allow them to stagger beyond periods into illiterate emotional fragments. Almost immediately I changed the subject noting that spring arrived in South Carolina earlier than in Connecticut. "The first shouts we'll hear won't be the lyric flutings of pan pipes. They'll be the bubbling whoops of amorous gray tree frogs. For years I mistakenly thought flickers made the cries calling to one another as they rummaged across dead trees," I said. "Now let me look at this autobiography," I continued, opening my friend's manuscript. "I was born 11 April 1936—a day I do not remember," the chapter began. "You won't be able to resist a beginning like that," Vicki said. Vicki was right. Not far down the first page, my friend stated that his memories really began in 1938 when he and his parents moved into an apartment on Bristol's South Street Extension. "I remember our getting a new rug for the living room: rich red with some sort of pattern," he wrote. "It probably made such a deep impression on me because I was so low to the ground." Clearly the rug was hooked. I was caught and went inside to my study. I sat at my desk and pondered how to introduce my friend's autobiography. "Because we can be robust and healthy on paper long after our bodies break and bend, literary folks our age never completely stop writing," a retired editor wrote me from assisted living. Be the editor correct or not, I wanted to write a puff for my friend's autobiography. I hoped to encourage readers to appreciate the beguiling nature of his account. Maybe they'd break free from the caustic news of the moment and patting a knee mumble, "Damn, this is spot on, the way to describe and explain life." Perhaps someone will scroll back through her years and think, "I was born on 13 February 1953. What I remember and don't remember are..."

About the Author

Sam Pickering is a native of Tennessee. He has written more than thirty books, but doesn't consider himself so much a writer as Vicki's husband, their children's father, a neighbor, and a white-haired guy who mows the lawn, rakes leaves, and shovels snow. He writes about what he bumps against and what bumps against him. He is a member of the Fellowship of Southern Writers, and although he "loves" the South and his memories of growing up in Nashville, he has lived most of his life in New England, teaching at the University of Connecticut. "Sam is," a friend who lives around the corner says, "our Montaigne, always around, always garrulous, and always writing."

In the photo, Vicki Pickering holds Little Sammy Pickering, Big Sammy looks on beside the Reedy River in Greenville, South Carolina.